P9-CSH-421

Spiritual Autobiography
of Charles de Foucauld

The

SPIRITUAL AUTOBIOGRAPHY

of

CHARLES DE FOUCAULD

Edited and annotated by

JEAN-FRANÇOIS SIX

Translated from the French

by J. Holland Smith

The Word Among Us Press
9639 Doctor Perry Road
Ijamsville, Maryland 21754

ISBN: 0-932085-77-6
www.wordamongus.org

Originally published in French as
Lettres et Carnets: Textes Présentés et Ordonnés par Jean-François Six
Published in English in 1964 as *Spiritual Autobiography of Charles de Foucauld*
by P. J. Kenedy & Sons

Copyright © Editions du Seuil, 1966

Published in 2003 by The Word Among Us Press by arrangement
with Georges Borchardt, Inc., New York, and Editions du Seuil

No part of this publication may be reproduced, stored in a retrieval system, or
transmitted in any form or by any means—electronic, mechanical, photocopy,
recording, or any other—except for brief quotations in printed reviews, without
the prior permission of the publisher.

Made and printed in the U.S.A.

Library of Congress Control No: 2003102446

FOREWORD

One man, following God's call to live the hidden and obscure life of Jesus at Nazareth, makes his home among the poor and abandoned in the Sahara desert. His life is difficult; no one joins him; he makes no converts to Christianity. Finally, he is killed by Muslim gunmen. Like Jesus, many would have judged his earthly life a failure.

Yet even before he died, a small group of people in France had been inspired to live out the ideals he espoused. Today, almost one hundred years later, thousands of people belonging to several different religious and lay groups seek to imitate Charles de Foucauld by living Jesus' "hidden" life at Nazareth. They seek to proclaim the Gospel not just with words, but with their whole lives.

The *Spiritual Autobiography of Charles de Foucauld* is unique in that it relates the story of this holy man's life through his own words. Arranged in chronological order, his letters, notes, journal entries, and meditations document Charles de Foucauld's amazing spiritual transformation, from his first encounter with Christ to his decision to live in the desert with the Tuaregs. His eloquent spiritual meditations reveal a passionate man on fire with God's love who seeks the Lord's will for his life—whatever the cost.

As you read this book, please keep in mind that Charles de Foucauld had no thoughts that his notes and letters would ever be published. His meditations were written primarily as an aid to prayer. (The sources of texts already published in French are given in the footnote to the selections, and a list of abbreviations used in the footnotes is provided on page five.) In addition, Part III of the book, which discusses his life in North Africa, should be understood in terms of the period in which it was written. Charles de Foucauld's comments about the Muslim religion were made in the context of his great desire to see the native people embrace Christ. His love for the Muslim people was demonstrated in his decision to live among them and befriend them.

Fr. Jean-François Six, editor of The *Spiritual Autobiography of Charles de Foucauld*, is a well-known and prolific French author. He is also general coordinator of the Union of the Brothers and Sisters of Jesus, Sodality of Charles de Foucauld, one of groups belonging to de Foucauld's spiritual "family."

Charles de Foucauld is a witness of love in action. His love compelled him to imitate Jesus at Nazareth, to live in the desert among the poor, to seek companions on this journey, and even to desire martyrdom. As we accompany him on his spiritual pilgrimage, may he show us how to proclaim the Gospel in the most ordinary circumstances of our lives.

The Word Among Us

CONTENTS

Contents

INTRODUCTION

WHO IS THIS CHARLES DE FOUCAULD, whom Pope John Paul II recently declared "Venerable"? Who is this brilliant scientist, assassinated in the middle of the Sahara desert, who is one of the great mystics, along with Thérèse of Lisieux, given to us by the Holy Spirit in our time? Who is this secular priest who died almost alone and who, nonetheless, is today regarded as an elder brother by thousands of people: lay and religious, bishops, priests, and even non-believers? Who is he?

We can learn something of him through the biographies written of him. We can also approach him more directly by reading what he himself has written throughout his life, in the thirty years of his "hidden life," from his conversion in 1886 to his death in 1916.

A "hidden life": this is the essence of his spirituality—to replicate the life of Jesus at Nazareth. It is a common life that has nothing flashy about it and no notoriety, the kind of life which mirrors, from time immemorial, the lives of the great majority of human beings from their birth to their death. Charles de Foucauld observed that Jesus, even before publicly announcing his Gospel, lived his life in intimate union with the Father, *Abba*, in a small village of three hundred inhabitants. Nazareth of Galilee is a locality, not pure and holy like Jerusalem but one "contaminated" by pagans, a place out of which nothing good could come (John 1:46).

Charles de Foucauld was impassioned by the hidden life of the Son of God made man. At first he sought to imitate his life literally by becoming an unknown resident of Nazareth for three years—from 1897 to 1900. He worked as a domestic servant who was so poor and silent that the street urchins of Nazareth mocked him and threw stones at him. He worked and prayed and sought help for his prayer by reading the Scriptures. He filled notebook after notebook with meditations on the Gospels, reflections in which his heart cried out his love for Jesus. Certain pages are ablaze with the fire of his love. Perhaps most famous is his fervent prayer of abandonment, which was inspired by Jesus' words on the cross—"Father, into your hands I commend my spirit" (pp. 95-96).

We also learn about the life of Charles de Foucauld through the letters he wrote to his spiritual father, with whom Charles had a profound bond. Abbé Huvelin was the French priest who had guided him to his conversion in 1886 and who was himself an authentic mystic. In this correspondence, we read about the evolutionary process which led Charles to leave Nazareth in order to nurture his desire as a priest to be the bearer of the Gospel and the Eucharist. He traveled to the place where, in his younger days while he was an unbeliever, he had gone as an eminently successful explorer: Morocco. But that country, on whose border he lived for a time, refused him entry.

He then plunged even farther south into the Sahara. He became a Tuareg with Tuaregs, learning their ways and their language, which he transcribed in meticulously wrought dictionaries. He converted no one. He was there among these people as a visitor extending friendship, hoping that his presence would allow the Spirit to work silently, "perhaps for centuries." This attitude—one of extreme silence and solitude yet also made up of multiple encounters of welcome and respect for others—was in no way a passive stance. Charles de Foucauld was a man of action, not an ethereal contemplative.

Immediately after he arrived in North Africa as a priest in 1901, he protested vigorously against slavery, a practice still tolerated by the French authorities in Algeria, which was then a French colony. In 1907, Charles wrote to Abbé Huvelin, describing a situation in which the native people were being abandoned and for whom "next to nothing is being done." Charles de Foucauld believed in progress and development for these regions; and he witnessed the Europeans settled there ignoring the local people, living apart from them, and viewing them "always as foreigners and most of the time as enemies." This rejection of the native population deeply upset him, and he ardently urged his fellow Frenchmen "to do our duty towards them as good brothers" (p. 175). He desired to be viewed by all, whoever they were, as a true brother.

What could he do? He entertained the notion that some great writer would make the problem known. At the same time he envisioned lay Christians—artisans, small shopkeepers, and farmers—coming to live in French colonies where the Gospel was unknown to support the work of the missionaries there. They would carry out their work in an evangelical spirit, simply as Jesus did in Nazareth, "drawing unbelievers to the faith by their example, goodness and friendship" (p. 183).

For the benefit of these lay persons, as well as for priests living in non-Christian lands, he thought about creating a spiritual grouping or "brotherhood" destined to live an intensely Christian life and to promote a return to the Gospel. At his death, this "brotherhood" numbered only forty-eight members, half of whom were priests and half lay persons who had pledged themselves, in their diverse circumstances and professions, to live the life of Nazareth according to the "Gospel counsels" which Charles de Foucauld has proposed to them. But no one joined him in the Sahara.

At his death, one of these members, Louis Massignon, a French scholar of Islam, arranged for the writing of a biography which would make Charles de Foucauld known. He also published the *Gospel Counsels,* which are the heart and soul of what Charles de Foucauld has written—his legacy. [1]

Louis Massignon also served as the primary reference for the initial groupings and congregations which were founded based on the ideals and spirituality of Charles de Foucauld. Before his death, Louis

Massignon spoke of this brotherhood or "union" as a "sodality," a designation that signifies brotherhood. Today more than one thousand members living in more than fifty countries belong to the Sodality. They pray and work wherever they find themselves, imitating Jesus in his "hidden life" in Nazareth, united in the Communion of the Saints. [2]

The life of Charles de Foucauld is the story of a grain of wheat cast to the ground, sewn in the desert at the dawn of the twentieth century—an age characterized by an intense search for fraternity but also by enormous violations of human dignity. The thousands of men and women who today are Charles de Foucauld's disciples desire, as he did, to work for greater justice and peace in the world. They look to Charles de Foucauld—who viewed Jesus as his "beloved brother"—as their elder brother. These men and women have, in the Spirit, heard the call that Charles de Foucauld continues to proclaim today. They seek to become, increasingly and with each passing day, universal brothers and sisters to all whom they meet.

> Jean-François Six
> Paris
> March 2003

---

[1] Charles de Foucauld, *Conseils Evangeliques*, Paris, Seuil.

[2] Comprised of persons "of every condition, single or married, ecclesiastical or lay, committed to practice, all according to their respective vocations, the Gospel counsels." The Union of the Brothers and Sisters of Jesus, Sodality of Charles de Foucauld (The Union-Sodality) is structured not along lines of nationality but of language, this in accord with the spirit of Pentecost. In addition to informal gatherings, a newsletter is the link among them and can be ordered via e-mail at UnionSodalite@aol.com. Information about other groups associated with Charles de Foucauld, such as the Little Brothers and Little Sisters of Jesus and several lay fraternities, can be found at the Web site www.jesuscaritas.info.

ABBREVIATIONS USED IN THE FOOTNOTES

AS	G. Gorrée:	*Les Amitiés Sahariennes du P. de Foucauld*, Arthaud, Grenoble, 1946.
B	R. Bazin:	*Charles de Foucauld, Explorateur du Maroc, Eremite au Sahara*, Plon, Paris, 1921.
C		*Père de Foucauld—Abbé Huvelin, Correspondance inédite*, Desclée, Tournai, 1957.
ES		*Ecrits spirituels de Charles de Foucauld*, Gigord, Paris, 1923.
FMS	Father Chauler:	*Père de Foucauld et Mère Saint Michel*, Saint Paul, Paris, 1946.
IS	J.-F. Six:	*Itinéraire Spirituel de Charles de Foucauld*, Seuil, Paris, 1958.
LHC		*Charles de Foucauld, Lettres à Henry de Castries*, Grasset, Paris, 1938.
NES		*Charles de Foucauld, Nouveaux Ecrits Spirituels*, Plon, Paris, 1950.
OS		*Frère Charles de Jésus, Oeuvres Spirituelles, Anthologie*, Seuil, Paris, 1958.
RPV	R. Pottier:	*La Vocation Saharienne du Père de Foucauld*, Plon, Paris, 1939.
TPF	G. Gorrée:	*Sur les Traces du Père de Foucauld*, La Colombe, Paris, 1953.

PART ONE

From his conversion (October 29, 1886)
to his arrival
in Nazareth (March 1897)

*C*harles de Foucauld was born at Strasbourg on September 15, 1858, and lost his parents when he was six years old. His childhood was very religious and he made a fervent first Holy Communion.

In the course of his studies at Nancy he lost the faith under the influence—among other things—of the generally agnostic atmosphere. His apostasy was quickly followed by a general moral collapse.

He joined the army and continued to be loose-living and idle. In March 1881, when he was with his regiment in Algeria, he was discharged for "ignominious conduct." After a few months of scandalous living he pulled himself together and reenlisted in the army.

In Africa he was fascinated by another project—that of exploring unknown and hostile Morocco. At the age of twenty-five he showed extraordinary courage in doing so. He then returned to France and, working alone, prepared an account of his explorations. It was at this time—the end of October 1886—that he was converted.

It was a total conversion and occurred while he was making his confession to the Abbé Huvelin, priest-in-charge at St. Augustine's in Paris. "Immediately I came to believe there was a God," he said later, "I saw I could not do anything except live for him; my religious vocation was born at the same moment as my faith." [1]

---

[1] From a letter to his friend Henry de Castries, dated September 14, 1901 (cf. IS, p. 38).

9

He wanted to enter the religious life immediately, but to make him more flexible and patient, the Abbé Huvelin directed him to wait for three years. While meditating on the mercies of God in the solitude of his tiny hermitage at Nazareth in November 1897, eleven years after his conversion, he told the story of his youth and conversion, his admission to La Trappe and departure seven years later for Nazareth and the hidden life he longed to share with Christ in his poverty:

O Lord Jesus, guide my thoughts and my words. If in my earlier meditations I showed my powerlessness, how much the more I do so now in these! It is not that I lack subjects for meditation; on the contrary, I am crushed with the weight of them. How many are your mercies, O God—mercies yesterday and today, and at every moment of my life, from before my birth, from before time itself began! I am plunged deep in mercies—I drown in them: they cover me, wrapping me round on every side.

O God, we should all hymn the praises of your mercies—we, who were all created for everlasting glory and redeemed by the blood of Jesus, by your blood, my Lord Jesus, beside me now in the tabernacle. But if we all have cause to do so, then how much the more have I? From my childhood I have been surrounded by so many graces: the son of a saintly mother, who learned from her to know you, to love you, and, as soon as I could speak at all, to pray to you. My first recollection is of the prayer she made me say night and morning: "God bless mama and papa, and grandmama and grandpapa Foucauld, and my little sister."

And the true piety of my upbringing! The visits to churches, the flowers laid at the foot of the cross, the Christmas crib, the month of Mary, the little altar in my room that stayed there as long as I had a room of my own there, even outliving my faith; the catechisms, the first confessions guided by my Christian grandfather, the examples of true devotion given me by my family. I see myself going to church with my father (and how long ago that is!), and with my grandfather. I see grandmother and my cousins going to Mass every day. And my first Holy Communion, after a long and careful preparation, surrounded by the blessings and encouragement of a family wholly Christian, in the presence of those I loved best in all the world, so that on a single day there came together everything necessary to let me taste pure joy.

And then my further instruction, under the direction of a good, holy, intelligent, zealous priest, with my grandfather always there, encouraging me in the path of devotion by word and example; the souls of my family, so devout and lovely, filling me with encouragement and goodness, and you, O God, causing to take root in my heart an attachment to them so deep that no later storms could uproot it—an attachment that later you were to be able to use to save me when I was as one dead, drowned in evil.

And then, when alas, despite so many blessings, I began to drift away from you, how gently you used my grandfather's voice to call me back to you. With what mercy you restrained me from falling into the ultimate excesses by keeping tenderness towards him alive in my heart. But alas, in spite of everything, I withdrew even further from you, my Lord and my Life, and my life began to be a death, or rather, had already become a death in your eyes.

Yet in that state of death, you preserved me still, keeping the memories of past times alive in my soul, together with esteem for what was good, and an attachment, dormant yet still alive like the glow of fire under the ashes, to certain beautiful and devout souls, and respect for the Catholic faith and the religious life. All my faith had vanished, but respect and esteem were still there, untouched. And you gave me other graces too, O God: you kept alive in me the taste for study, for serious reading and good things, and with it a disgust for vice and shame. I did evil, but I never approved of it or loved it.

You made me experience a melancholic emptiness, a sadness

that I never felt at other times. It would come back to me every evening when I was alone in my rooms; it kept me silent and depressed during our so-called celebrations: I would organize them, but when the time came, I went through them in silence, disgust and infinite boredom. You gave me the ill-defined unrest that marks an unquiet conscience which, though it may be wholly asleep, is not completely dead. I never felt that sadness, that distress, that restlessness apart from those times. It was undoubtedly a gift from you, O God. How far off I was in my doubting! How good you are!

While through this device of your love you were preventing my soul from being unredeemably overwhelmed, you were also protecting my body: if I had died then I should have gone to hell—the accidents on horseback miraculously avoided; the duels you prevented from taking place; the perils of war from which you saved me; the perils of travel, so great and so many, from which you delivered me as though by a miracle; my unfailing health in so many pestiferous places, and despite my being so overtired. O God, how firmly you have kept your hand on me, and how little I have felt it! How good you are: how you have protected me! How truly you covered me with your wings when I did not even believe you existed!

And while you were thus protecting me, time passed, until the moment came when you judged it right to bring me back into the fold. In spite of me, you dissolved all the evil relationships that would have kept me away from you. You even unloosed all those good ties that would have prevented me from returning to the bosom of my family, where you willed that I should find salvation, but which would have prevented me from one day living for you alone. At the same time, you gave me a life of serious studies, an obscure life in solitude and poverty. In heart and mind I was still far from you, yet I had begun to live in a less vicious atmos-

phere; it was neither true light nor goodness—that was lacking—
·but it was not so deep a morass nor so odious a wickedness. Little
by little the place was swept clean; the flood still covered the
earth, but the waters were continually falling, and it had stopped
raining. You had broken down the barriers, softened my soul, prepared the ground by burning off the thorns and bushes.

By the force of events, you made me be chaste, and soon, at
the end of the winter of 1886, when you had guided me back to
my family in Paris, chastity became a blessing and inner necessity
to me. It was you who did that, O God—you alone. I, alas, had
no part in it. How good you have been! From what sad and cul-
pable relapses you miraculously preserved me! Your hand alone
has done this—at the beginning, midway, and at the end. How
good you are! My soul had to be made ready to receive the truth:
the devil is too much the master of an unchaste soul to let truth
enter it. You could not, O God, come into a soul where the devil
of unbridled passions ruled supreme. But you wanted to come into
my soul, O Good Shepherd, and you yourself expelled your enemy
from it. And having expelled him by force, in spite of me, seeing
my weakness and how little capable I was of keeping my soul pure
for myself, you set a vigilant watchman over it, a watchman so
strong and yet so gentle that not only did he prevent the devil of
impurity from entering it in the least degree, but he also made
the delights of chastity a need and blessing to me. O my God,
how shall I hymn your mercies?

And having cleansed the filth from my soul and entrusted it to
your angels, you, O God, planned to reenter it yourself—for even
after having received so many graces, it still did not acknowledge
you. You were working in it and upon it continually, transforming
it with sovereign power and astonishing speed—and still it ignored
you completely. Then you breathed into it a taste for virtue, the
virtue of the pagans: you let me search through the works of the

pagan philosophers, and I found nothing there but emptiness and disgust. Next you let me glance at a few pages of a Christian book, and you made me conscious of its warmth and beauty. You made me realize that I might find there, if not truth (for I did not believe that men can know truth), at least the elements of virtue, and you inspired me to look for instruction in a virtue completely pagan in Christian books. Thus you brought to me an awareness of the mysteries of religion.

At the same time, you were continually strengthening the bonds uniting me with lofty souls: you led me back to the family to which I had been so warmly attached in former years, in the time of my childhood. You let me rediscover my former admiration for these same souls, and you inspired them to receive me as a prodigal son who is not made even to feel that he had ever left his father's house, giving them the same goodness towards me I might have expected if I had never failed them. I became ever more firmly bound to my beloved family. Among them I lived in such an atmosphere of virtue that my life visibly became again what it had been: spring was giving life back to the earth after the winter, and this gentle sun made my longing for good grow, together with distaste for evil, the impossibility of falling back into certain faults, and a search for goodness. You expelled evil from my heart; my good angel took its place there once again, and you associated a terrestrial angel with it.

By the beginning of October 1886, after six months of family life, I admired virtue and longed for it, but I still did not know you. By what devices, O God of goodness, you made yourself known to me! What devices did you not use? What exterior means, both gentle and strong? What an astonishing series of circumstances, in which everything combined to drive me towards you: unexpected solitude, my emotions, the sickness of those dear to me, ardent feelings, a return to Paris as the result of a surprising event. And what interior graces: the need for solitude, recollection and pious reading; the urge I felt to go into your churches—I who did not believe in you; my unrest of soul, my anguish; my search for truth; my prayer: "O God, if you exist, let me know of your existence." All these things were your work, O God—the work of you alone.

A noble soul supported you—by its silence, its gentleness, its goodness and perfection. It let itself be seen; it was good and it spread its seductive perfume around itself, but it never intruded itself. It was you, O Jesus, my Saviour, who did all things, both within and without. You attracted me to virtue through a soul in which virtue seemed so beautiful to me that it snatched away my heart irrecoverably. Through that same soul, you also attracted me to truth. Then you gave me four blessings. First you inspired me with the thought that as this soul was so intelligent, the religion it believed so firmly could not be the folly I had thought it. Second, you inspired me with another idea: since this religion is not folly, may it not be that there is to be found in it that truth which is to be found in no other upon earth, nor yet in any system of philosophy?

Your third blessing was to say to me: Study this religion, then— put yourself under a teacher of the Catholic religion, a learned priest, and see what there is in it, and if you find yourself compelled to believe what it teaches. And the fourth was the unparalleled blessing of directing me for my instruction in religion to Father Huvelin. I believe, O God, that by leading me to go into his confessional on one of the last days of that October (between the 27th and the 30th) you were giving me the best of all good things. If there is joy in heaven at the repentance of a sinner, then how great joy there must have been when I entered his confessional! What a blessed day that was—a day of blessing. And since that day my whole life has been a chain of blessings.

You put me under the wing of a saint, and I have stayed there. You used his hands to bear me up, and the result has been grace upon grace. I asked for instruction in religion: he made me get down on my knees and make my confession and sent me straight away to Holy Communion. When I think of it, I cannot stop myself from crying: and I do not want to stop the tears running down for, O God, they are so justified. What streams of tears should flow from my eyes at the remembrance of so many mercies! How good you have been—how happy I am! What have I done to deserve it?

Since then, O God, there has been an unbroken chain of ever growing graces. They have been an ever-rising sea: direction—and what direction!—prayer, sacred reading, daily attendance at Mass established from the first days of my new life; frequent Communion, frequent confession after the passage of a few weeks; direction that became ever more personal and frequent, embracing the whole of my life, making it a life of obedience in the smallest things—and obedience to what a master! Communion became almost a daily occurrence; my nascent longing for the religious life grew stronger. External events, independent of my will, compelled me to detach myself from the material things which held so much charm for me, and which would have held back my soul, keeping it chained to the world. You broke these bonds violently, as you had broken so many others.

How good you are, my God, to have broken everything around me, to have annihilated in such a way everything that would have prevented me living for you alone, giving me an ever deeper feeling of the futility and falseness of the life of the world, and of the vast distance there is between the perfect life, the life of the Gospel, and the life men lead in the world. You gave me a tender and increasing love for you, O Lord Jesus, and a taste for prayer, trust in your word, a profound awareness of the duty of almsgiving, a longing to imitate you. You gave me too those words in a sermon of Father Huvelin's which are now so indelibly engraved on my soul: "May you so truly have taken the lowest place, that no one will ever be able to take it from you," and a thirst to give you the greatest sacrifice I am capable of making for you, by leaving forever the family which had been all my joy, to live and die far away from it. You gave me my search for a life like yours, in which I might share completely in your abjection, your poverty, your humble work, your obscurity—the search made so clear to me in a last retreat at Clamart.

On January 15, 1890, I was enabled to make this sacrifice, and I received from your hand that grace, La Trappe: daily Communion; all I learned in seven years spent in the religious life; the graces of Our Lady of the Snows; the graces of Nôtre Dame du Sacré Cœur; the graces of Staouëli; the graces of Rome, the city of St. Peter and the martyrs, with its basilicas and churches, its countless traces of the apostles and martyrs, theology, philosophy, lectures, the exceptional vocation to a life of poverty and obscurity.

After three and a half years spent in waiting, the most reverend General told me, on January 23, 1897, that it was the will of God that I should follow that in me which was driving me out of the Trappist Order into a life of poverty, humble labor and profound obscurity—the life whose vision had been with me so long. There followed my departure for the Holy Land, my pilgrimage and arrival at Nazareth. The first Wednesday I spent there you led me, O God, through the intercession of St. Joseph, to enter the convent of St. Clare as a servant. O the peace, happiness, consolation, blessings, and wonderful happiness I knew there! *Misericordias Domini in aeternum cantabo. . . . Venite et videte, quoniam suavis est Dominus.*[2]

I can only fall far short of such mercies, O God: I can only

[2] "The mercies of the Lord I will sing for ever. . . . O taste and see that the Lord is sweet."

beseech the Blessed Virgin and all devout souls to give thanks for me, for I am overwhelmed by blessings. O beloved Bridegroom, what have you not done for me? What do you want from me? What do you expect from me, that you have so overwhelmed me? O God, give yourself thanks through me, create remembrance, gratitude, fidelity and love in me; I am overcome, I fail, O God; create my thoughts, words and deeds, so that they may all give you thanks and glorify you in me. Amen. Amen. Amen.[3]

So, then, on January 15, 1890, Charles de Foucauld left Paris, his people and his place in the world, to shut himself away in the Trappist monastery of Our Lady of the Snows (in the department of Ardèche). It was a great sacrifice on his part. On January 16 he wrote:

. . . I must draw strength from my weakness, using that very weakness itself for God, thanking him for this pain, offering it to him. I beseech him with all my heart to increase my pain if I can bear any more, that he may draw a little consolation from it, and his children may have a little more of what is good from it; may he lessen it if it is not for his glory and according to his will—but I am certain that he who wept for Lazarus does will it. . . .[4]

And on February 6:

In this sad world, there is a joy at the heart of things which is not shared by either the saints in heaven or the angels—that of suffering with our Beloved. However hard life may be, however

---

[3] Notes on the Retreats at Nazareth, no. 14; cf. ES, pp. 159–67.
[4] From a letter to his cousin, Madame de Bondy (cf. TPS, p. 72 ff.).

long our days of sadness may endure, however consoling the thought of the pleasant valley of Josaphat may be, we must never seek to leave the foot of the cross sooner than God would have us do. The good cross, St. Andrew called it. Our Master having been good enough to let us experience, if not always its sweetness, then at least its beauty and necessity for those who love him, we do not want to be freed from it any quicker than it is his will we should be. And yet God knows the day this exile ends will be a welcome one, for there is more strength in my words than in my heart.[5]

Why then did he enter the Trappist Order? He gave his reasons to a friend on April 24 of that year:

Out of your dear friendship for me, you ask me: Why did I enter La Trappe? I did so from love, from pure love. I love our Lord Jesus Christ, though it be with a heart that wishes to love more and more perfectly; yet I love him, and I can bear to lead no life but his, a sweet and honorable life, notwithstanding that it was the hardest and most lowly there has ever been.[6]

On June 26 he left Our Lady of the Snows for a daughter house, the Trappist monastery of Nôtre Dame du Sacré Cœur, near Akbès in Syria. He had asked to be sent to this far-off monastery, which was poorer than any of the others, before he entered Our Lady of the Snows. At Nôtre Dame du Sacré Cœur, Foucauld continued his novitiate under the direction of the sub-prior, Father Polycarp.
He had entered La Trappe in order to lead a life resembling as

---

[5] From a letter to Madame de Bondy (cf. TPF, p. 74).
[6] From a letter to H. Duveyrier (cf. RPV, p. 52).

closely as possible the life of Jesus at Nazareth. But wretched as it was, this Trappist house at Akbès was still not poor enough for him. On October 30 he wrote to the Abbé Huvelin:

You express the hope that I now have poverty enough. But no. To the rich, we are poor, but we are not poor as our Lord was, not as poor as I was in Morocco, not as poor as St. Francis. . . . I regret it, without letting it worry me: in this respect, too, I maintain silence and obedience. Little by little, without drawing attention to myself, and especially after my profession—if God lets me live so long—I shall be able to obtain dispensations that will allow me at least to practise poverty more perfectly; for the moment, I keep silent.[7]

On December 15 he wrote to the same priest:

Soon the year '90 will go to join those that have already flowed away—the dear year '90, of which the first fortnight is so firmly embedded in my memory, so full of emotions and pains, while the rest is so generously filled with divine graces. The year '90, when I put so much behind me, and was given so much: the holy habit, the wedding garment given by our Lord to one so unworthy; this marvelous peace in which it has pleased him to keep me uninterruptedly. Give thanks on my behalf, M. l'Abbé: give thanks for the infinite graces of that first fortnight of January in the year '90, days so dear to my heart, so full of memories, in which you played so large a part, days so full of the very goodness of God himself, so blessed by so many divine favors. Give thanks for my first eleven months in the religious life, where God has put me into so admirable a state of peace that I could not fail to be inspired to great gratitude, readiness and faith. Thank him

[7] Cf. C, p. 5 ff.

too for the good you have done me, for the sight of the other novices compels me to thank him constantly for being prepared by you for the life we are leading. I am gathering the fruits of your preparation, and I am conscious of all I owe to the dear hand with which you labored in so poor a soil. . . .

There is nothing remarkable, nothing new in my soul. I live from one day to the next with our Lord, the most holy Virgin, the saints I know best, and those I love: you know that you are one of them. I give thought neither to tonight nor to tomorrow. I sometimes remember that the day will come when there will be no tomorrow in this world. And that is my life.[8]

On September 16, 1891, he wrote again to the same priest:

How paternal His hand has been! Could He save me by a more gentle means? It is not for me to forget that we have a Father in heaven. I must always proclaim it, and always have confidence. What have you not been to me, both in the time immediately after my conversion, during the years that followed, and indeed always? If I should remember that I have a Father in heaven, I am no less conscious of having a father on earth. By the grace of God, it was the same hand that directed me to both my fathers: may God be praised; may that hand be blessed; may you be blessed!

It was twenty months ago yesterday that I said good-bye to you in Paris and two years since I left La Barre at the end of my pleasant stay there. Yesterday was my thirty-third birthday. Pray God that this new year may be used truly in his love and service, that in it I may do the good I did not do last year, and lastly that I may be a brave and loyal servant, a loving and most obedient son—in short, that I may do his will, for that is everything. Another four months and the day I take my vows will be here. It

[8] Cf. C, pp. 9 & 11.

will be a great day for us—I say "us" because I am your child and you will surely be thinking of me. It will most probably be on the second of February, but it is not certain.

My life is unchanged: divided between work and prayer. I do almost no reading: I spend almost all my free time in church. Father Polycarp does not stop me—on the contrary. Since our Lord is there, what else should I do? My spiritual life has not changed: it is filled with the presence of our Lord, and of his beloved saints who were with him on earth, and is one with that of those I love so much in this world. In such pleasant company the days pass quickly and I can do nothing but give thanks to God. He has continued to give me the grace he has shown me ever since my first days in the monastery; it increases rather than lessens, and my peace too is growing—by the grace of God I find it in front of the tabernacle.

He is there, so what more do I need? And he is perfectly happy there, so should I not be happy? Yet—I am not, for those I love in this world are suffering, or are disturbed and unhappy. I pray to him for them, very unworthily, but with all that is in my heart. Praying to our Lord for those I love is the chief business of the hours I spend at his feet—when I do what I can both for him and for them—and that is all that needs to be done.[9]

On November 28, 1892, he gave an account of his life to his cousin Louis de Foucauld. In it already appears the emphasis he was to put all his life on the necessity for the apostolate of the inner conversion of the apostle himself.

Our district is a nest of robbers. It is we who must shape the future for these peoples. The future—the only real future—is

[9] Cf. C, p. 19 ff.

eternal life: this life is only a short trial, preparing us for that to come. The conversion of these peoples is in God's hands—both theirs and ours, the Christians. God always gives his grace abundantly; they are free to accept or reject the faith. Preaching is difficult in Moslem lands, but the missionaries of so many past centuries overcame many other difficulties. Our task is to be the successors to the first apostles and evangelists. The word is mighty, but example, love and prayer are a thousand times more so. We must give them the example of a perfect life, of a higher and holy life; we must love them with the all powerful love that draws love; we must pray for them with hearts warm enough to bring down upon them a superabundance of divine grace. Then we cannot fail to convert them.[10]

On February 7, he wrote to a Trappist:

For us, rest is to be found in rejoicing in the infinite goodness of God and, looking a little lower, in finding joy in our crosses, and ever longing to bear them better, for, in doing so, we have the joy of imitating Him and proving our love for Him—things so dear to the loving heart. We shall never lack either joy, or God, or yet crosses . . .[11]

His life continued. More and more Charles de Foucauld (or, as he was called in religion, Brother Marie-Albéric) detached himself from La Trappe. During this same period there began to grow in his mind the longing to found a congregation himself.
In August 1892, he was started on a course in theology.
In November, he fell ill, and remained sick for quite a long

[10] Cf. B, pp. 114 ff.
[11] From a letter of Father Eugen, dated February 7, 1893 (cf. ES, p. 2).

time. *"But I cannot hope to go this time: to tell you I do not want to would be a lie,"* *he wrote to Madame de Bondy.*[12]

The course in theology was resumed in February, but Brother Marie-Albéric expressed a firm desire not to receive priestly orders.

In June the Trappists of Akbès received their new rules and constitutions. To Brother Marie-Albéric they did not appear to call for the degree of poverty he longed to see.

Several letters to the Abbé Huvelin explain his state of mind.

June 14, 1893

They tell me, Monsieur l'Abbé, that you are better—at least you are no worse, and that is good to know. You know very well that it makes me unhappy to have to be pleased with so little for you and to have to be happy on your account with a state of health that many another would find miserable. May God guard and guide you! I dare not be unhappy about the weight of the cross laid on you by his hand, for he loves you more than I can, even though I am your child. And he will reward you so richly. Yet I cannot see you suffer without being distressed. May the will of God be fulfilled for you and me and all those we love. . . .

Now what of me and my soul? Your child's soul is still unchanged, Monsieur l'Abbé, still full of tenderness towards you, but still full also of meanness, pride, vanity, trust in my own judgment, harshness towards others and indulgence towards myself, cowardice, timorousness; it is still, alas, devoid of charity. I am lukewarm, distracted, lacking in both gratitude and repentance. These are my chief faults; they are not the only ones, but I will spare you the rest. God still preserves my peace: he is still giving me the gentle life of the soul, keeping me always mindful of him, of the Blessed Virgin, and of those he has given me to love best. This is the foundation of my life. Outwardly, there have been

[12] In a letter written at the end of November 1892 (Cf. TPF, p. 84).

some changes: I am willingly studying a little theology, but do so in the hope of always remaining what I am. I am unhappy to say I am no longer sawing wood, but I still ring the bells and act as sacristan. My health is perfect—it has never been better. But sometimes I am a little worried about myself. . . . Help me: set me on fire again. Do not let me lose the love for our Lord you put in my heart, with all that was in you and with so much care.

I want then to ask your advice. You know that before novices are admitted to profession, the Superior asks the guidance of the community, who vote black or white. Should those novices be accepted who have genuine virtues and seem likely never to give the community trouble, but who otherwise seem to seek only some indefinable ideal of religious life which is peaceful, pious and easy, having all that is necessary and not a little besides, and who never follow the rule without mitigations either requested by themselves or accepted happily by them? Or should we accept only those who appear to be determined to seek our Lord cost what it may, following the rule and walking with our first fathers in the footsteps of our Lord himself? These questions will not give you a high opinion of our loyalty to the rule, I am afraid, Monsieur l'Abbé.

Alas! Pray for your child, Monsieur l'Abbé. I know very well that you do so, for if I, wretch that I am, think of you constantly, how should you not remember me? Write to me, too, when you can do so without getting over-tired; it would do me good—I need it. I often receive news of you in letters that do me infinite good. Bless me, Monsieur l'Abbé. And bless her, too, who has done so much for me. Your blessing is too precious for me not to want to share it with her.

Your most respectful and devoted child in Jesus Christ, our Lord

Brother Marie-Albéric [13]

---

[13] Cf. C, pp. 24 ff.

July 8, 1893

The feast of St. Henry is nearly upon us, Monsieur l'Abbé, and I am already late in offering you my good wishes for your feast. I hope, however, that on that day you will realize that your child in Syria has not forgotten you and remembers the day—although I am sure you do realize it, I still like to tell you this. That day I shall pray for you even more than usual, and although my prayers may be nothing, I hope that, as God bids me be grateful and loving, he will hear the prayers he has himself inspired. Besides, what could I ask of him other than what he himself wills for you? And as what I want to ask from him for you is the highest good, what better thing could I ask than that there may be done in you the Will of him whose love for you is infinite and who knows what is best for you?

The last news I had of you was that you were a little better: at least, you were no worse. I hope that your health is not too bad now. I say 'I hope'—I mean rather I long so with all my heart, for at this distance, with letters taking so long, one cannot count on knowing how people are. One has to put oneself in God's hands and pray to him for those one loves. Pray, then, for me, for I am most wretched, cowardly and lukewarm, not very obedient, or rather, I obey badly, and sometimes I am a little concerned about what I see *not* being practiced around me—those virtues which should be there—and also by what I see of the spirit of the world enthroned among us all, although it should be so far from us. What a beautiful and blessed and divine thing is poverty, and how repulsive it is to human beings.

We have received details of our new *Us*—not definitive yet, but experimental. The next General Chapter will make them definitive, amending them where necessary. They are devout and austere: that is one consolation; it is a *reform,* not the *deformation* I feared. And reform really is needed—but I do not think the change will be a profound one. It does not go to the bottom of things, and it is at the foundation that we are sinning. We are not based on a sufficiently genuine poverty; not being satisfied with what is absolutely necessary, one is obliged, in order to have extra, to have recourse to a thousand stratagems, which quickly afford an entry to dissipation—and when one seeks a path different from our Lord's, one runs a strong risk of going astray. . . .

Forgive this hasty letter, Monsieur l'Abbé. Its only purpose is to tell you again what you already know: that your child loves you, with a respectful, but also most tender affection. Bless him from afar; and not him alone.

Your humble son in our Lord Jesus Christ,

Brother Marie-Albéric [14]

On August 26, 1893, Brother Marie-Albéric wrote a letter to his cousin, Madame de Bondy, in which he voiced his disquiet: the Order he had entered seemed to be continually moving further from the poverty and humility he was seeking. In a letter to Father Huvelin he outlined for the first time his plans for the foundation of a new Congregation.

September 22, 1893

It is a long time since I wrote to you, Monsieur l'Abbé, and if it were possible I should come and ring your doorbell and have a talk with you. "And—your soul?"—that would be your first question. It seems to me that it has not changed a great deal. It is still living on what you put into it. It still loves those it used to love—loving them more than formerly, rather than less. It is still full of wretchedness, and devoid of humility and simplicity. It is still too obstinately fixed on its own ideas, and certainly too cowardly in its actions. . . .

By the command of the Holy Father, some very good changes

[14] Cf. C, pp. 27–9.

have been made in our Order, but these changes and improvements will not stop the evil from growing. They will give greater unity to the Order and to some degree stop the individual Abbots from doing just as they like, and they will raise the standard of priestly studies. But we are turning ever more completely and further away from the poverty and the humility of the lowly life of Nazareth that I came here to seek, and from which I am infinitely far from being deterred—a life I am deeply troubled to see our Lord living alone, without a single soul or a single group in the Church today dreaming of living it with him, and sharing, for love of him and in his love, in the blessedness of the most holy Virgin and St. Joseph.

Is there no way of forming a little congregation to lead that life, living solely by the labor of its own hands—as did our Lord, who supported himself neither by alms nor offerings? Would it be impossible to find a few souls ready to follow our Lord in this— to follow him by following *all* his precepts, totally renouncing all property, collective no less than individual, and thus putting aside what our Lord himself rejected—all legal matters, conflicts and troubles, making an absolute duty of almsgiving—when they have two coats, giving one away, when they have food, giving to those who have none, keeping nothing back for the morrow; following all the examples set by his hidden life and all the precepts uttered by his lips? A life of work and prayer, not with two kinds of religious, as there are at Citeaux, but one, as St. Benedict wanted— but not using St. Benedict's complicated liturgy, but long hours of prayer, the rosary, the holy Mass. Our liturgy closes the doors of our monasteries to Arabs, Turks, Armenians and so on, who are good Catholics but do not know a word of our languages. I so long to see such small "nests" of men living an ardent and hard-working life, reproducing our Lord's own, established under his protection and under the guardianship of Mary and Joseph, close to all the mission stations of the East, now so isolated, so that they could offer refuge to the souls of the peoples of these countries called by God to serve him and love him alone.

Is it a dream, Monsieur l'Abbé—a diabolical illusion? Or is it an idea, or an invitation, sent from God? If I knew that it came from God, I would take the first steps necessary to lead me by that path today, not waiting till tomorrow. When I think about it, I find it a wonderful idea—to follow the example and counsels of our Lord could not fail to be an excellent thing. Moreover, it is exactly what I have always been seeking. It was precisely to find him that I came to La Trappe. It is not a new vocation. If such a company of souls had been in existence a few years ago I should—as you are aware—have gone straight to it. As there is no such thing, or anything approaching it, or anything to replace it, ought not an attempt to be made to form it? And to form it in the hope that one would see it grow especially in lands without the faith—Moslem and others?

I repeat: when I consider it, I find it perfect. But when I look at him to whom this idea came—and came so burning bright!—I cannot see in him, this sinner, this weak and wretched being you know, the material God would ordinarily use in making something good. He uses good materials for making good things. It is true that, if the idea comes from God, once things were started it is for him to give the increase and he will soon send souls fit to be the first stones of his house—souls before whom I should inevitably return to the nothingness which is my true place. Another thing gives me the courage to undertake a task so unsuitable for a sinner and one with my weaknesses, and that is the fact that our Lord said that when one has sinned much, one must love much. So, now, Monsieur l'Abbé, do you think this comes from God?

I shall, as you know, be guided by your reply and your advice, for a father never stops being a father, especially you to me! You see how much I need you. For two months now this idea has been so strong in me that although I thought I could keep it from Father Polycarp, my confessor, I found myself telling him about it a fortnight ago, though with far fewer details than I have set down here. He advised me to let the idea lie dormant for a while, not thinking any more about it, until an occasion presented itself. That was exactly what I had thought to do, but the occasion will inevitably present itself in a little over a year when the time comes for my final vows; and it could come sooner, perhaps, at the time, still unannounced, of the next [canonical] visitation. It seems hard not to be able to disclose my mind to the Visitor. For the time being, I am trying not to think about it. But I am scarcely succeeding. In any case, I had to tell you, and now it is done.

I am continuing with theology, very happy to be studying, and desiring more ardently than ever not to be raised to the priesthood. Four pages about myself—that saddens and frightens me! . . .

Bless me, Monsieur l'Abbé, and also those I love so much, praying that this letter may also bring them good.

Your loving son in our Lord Jesus Christ

Brother Marie-Albéric [15]

1894, 1895 and 1896 were years of agony to Brother Marie-Albéric. He thought constantly about the life of Nazareth, the life he longed to lead. Should he stay in the Trappist Order or not?

On June 14, 1896, he finished composing a Rule for the Congregation he wanted to found. He called its members the Hermits of the Sacred Heart.

He asked to be dispensed from his vows. In September 1896 he was sent for two years to Rome to study theology. He found

[15] Cf. C, pp. 30–4.

*it a new trial, especially as February 2, 1897 was appointed as
the day for him to take his final vows. Ought he to take them?
On December 21 he wrote to a Trappist friend:*

I do not want to let the holy season of Christmas go by without
telling you that during these blessed days I shall be as close as I
can be to you at the feet of our Lord Jesus.

Our Lord is now on the way to Bethlehem—the journey on foot
will probably take five days, the last of them only two or three
hours long: from Nazareth to Engannim, then to Sichar, then
Bethel, from Bethel to Jerusalem, and finally from Jerusalem to
Bethlehem. How full of love and recollection the Blessed Virgin
must have been when she made that journey. How she must have
burned with longing for the salvation of mankind, for whose sake
the Son of God had come down into her womb.

At every moment of the journey, our Lord saw not only his
Mother and St. Joseph, and the angels worshiping him, but also
this present time and the future, every moment in the life of every
human being. What is more, at the prospect of the sins, ingratitude
and damnation of so many souls, his sacred Heart was already ex-
periencing the terrible pain that was to be its lot throughout his
life on earth. Yet he also tasted, as well as the great consolation
afforded him by the holiness of his mother, a lesser, but still real,
consolation at the prospect of all the souls of the saints, all the
souls who had loved him and who would one day love him, all
the hearts that would join with Mary's in beating for him alone.
Shall we be among them, dear Father? Shall we be consolation
or pain to our blessed Saviour?

If Christmas marks the beginning of our joys, it is also the
beginning of Jesus' agonies. There are only eight days between
Christmas and the Circumcision. Bethlehem is only five miles from
Jerusalem. In Palestine one is made painfully aware of this fact:

having spent the Christmas of 1888 in Bethlehem, hearing midnight Mass and receiving Holy Communion in the cave, I returned to Jerusalem at the end of two or three days. The delight I had experienced at praying in the very cave which had echoed to the voices of Jesus, Mary and Joseph—the cave where I had been so close to them—was indescribable. But, alas, after an hour's traveling there rose up before me the dome of the Church of the Holy Sepulchre, Calvary and the Mount of Olives, and whether I wanted to or not, I was compelled to begin a new line of thought and go back to the foot of the cross.[16]

In a meditation at the end of December he set himself the problem of determining God's will, praying insistently for enlightenment.

Poverty, humbleness, penitence—you, O God, know my sole longing is to practise them to the extent and in the exact way you want me to do. But what are that way and degree? Before coming into the Order, and right up to now, I have always thought that I should practise them in your image, by imitating you as nearly as possible, by making myself follow, as far as I could, the way in which you yourself practised them. Now I am told I might be mistaken, that in fact such imitation of the divine Master is truly in itself the best, the most perfect way—but that perhaps you might not will this best way for me, that you are not calling me to so perfect a life, that you will not allow me to follow you so closely in this way. And indeed, O God, if I look at myself, there is such a gap between my wretchedness and true perfection; I am so unworthy of being counted among those privileged friends who follow you most closely, that it seems infinitely just

[16] From a letter to Father Jerome, dated from Rome on December 21, 1896 (cf. B, pp. 139 ff.).

to me that I should not have so unusually privileged a vocation.

But, on the other hand, you have heaped so many blessings upon me that I think it would be ungrateful to your Heart not to believe that it is prepared to heap every blessing, however great, upon me; not to believe that the love of your Heart, like its generosity, is beyond measure. So then, I can hardly believe that I am mistaken in my choice at this point (for if I am mistaken now, I was equally wrong earlier: I made the wrong choice and should not have entered the Trappist Order).

I find it hard to believe that I have been wrong in seeking you along this path for the last eight years; I find it hard to believe that the words *Estoti perfecti* and *Sequere me*[17] are not meant for all those who sincerely want to be your disciples, abandoning and renouncing everything, even themselves, for your sake. I find it especially hard to believe, O God, that you, who so far surpass us in generosity, would not give yourself most freely to those who give themselves wholly and unreservedly to you, having only one desire, to do always what would be most pleasing to you. I think I see my God clearly. Give me full enlightenment so that I may act in the certain knowledge of doing your will, for this is the food by which I long to live always. And grant, too, that I may only fear doing something other than what would give most glory to you. Amen.[18]

In another meditation on the Old Testament, he again reveals in himself the same search and the same hope.

It was *at the very time* when Jacob was traveling, poor and alone, and laid himself down on the ground naked in the desert

[17] "Be perfect" and "Follow me."
[18] From his "Meditations on the Old Testament," under Gen. 30:1–21 (cf. IS, pp. 181 ff.).

to rest after a long journey on foot, *at the very time* when he was in the unhappy position of being an isolated traveler in the middle of a long journey through a strange and desolate country, without shelter, *at the very time* when he found himself in this sad situation, that God heaped unparalleled favors upon him. Appearing to him in a wonderful vision in which, after showing him the angels continually watching over mankind, going constantly from earth to heaven and from heaven back to earth to bring men everything they need, he promised to protect him throughout his journey and heap graces upon him both during his life and after his death, blessing through one of his descendants all the nations of the earth, and causing the divine Son to be born into his family. He surrounded Jacob with such radiance and bliss that the poor traveler, who had been so exhausted and unhappy when he lay down, got up saying: "This is no other but the house of God and the gate of heaven."

After that, O God, who could be afraid of long journeys on foot, through the land of unknown peoples, in poverty and alone— especially if he were doing it for the sake of following you, of loving you more perfectly and serving you more fully? Who could be afraid when you so liberally pour out such delights on those who seem bound to suffer so many griefs? O my God, how easily you turn sorrow into joy, level mountains, and make things that seem almost impossible quite easy! "Seek first the kingdom of God . . . and all these things shall be added unto you." Let us do whatever is most perfect; if we undertake it, God will make it succeed. And when it is clear to us that the most perfect thing would be to undertake long journeys, alone and on foot, begging our bread with St. Peter, St. Paul and so many other saints, let us not be afraid to do so. We are never alone. Our guardian angels cover us with their wings. Jesus is in our hearts. God overshadows us. The eyes of the holy Virgin are upon us. And it is while we are on the very journeys that seem so miserable to us, that God makes us cry out: "This is the house of God and the gate of heaven." [19]

In the week of January 16–23, 1897, Brother Marie-Albéric abandoned himself utterly to God. He determined to do whatever his superiors should decide; if it meant that he must be a Trappist and become a priest, he would do so. Then, on January 23, the Father General of the Trappists confirmed that his vocation was to Nazareth, and suggested he should leave for Nazareth itself to follow his vocation humbly there.

The following day he told a Trappist friend, Father Jerome, about the act of abandonment the Lord had required of him, and how he had accepted it.

Rome, January 24, 1897

I believe my vocation is to humble myself . . . Every door has opened to me to make it possible for me to stop being a choir monk and go down to the level of a servant, a houseman. I received the news yesterday from the lips of our good and excellent Father General himself. I find his goodness towards me very moving. But when I had the most need of obedience was before he took this decision. I had promised God that I would do all the reverend Father told me to do after he had gone into the question of my vocation, and also whatever my confessor told me to do. Even if he had said, "In ten days' time you are to take your final vows and afterwards you will receive Holy Orders," I should have obeyed joyfully, certain that I was trying to do the will of God . . . And now I am no less in God's hands and under obedience. I asked where I should go when I leave here within a few days. I am to go to the East, but to which house I have no idea. God will tell me through the lips of my director . . . You

[19] Meditation on Gen. 28:11–22 (cf. OS, pp. 65 ff.).

will see that I need my brother's prayers. I shall be bringing you down, too, my most dear brother—there is nothing wonderful in the eyes of the world in being the brother of a servant, a domestic, a houseman. But you have died to the world, and nothing can make you blush.

Thank you for opening your heart to me about your longing for priestly orders. I give thanks to God with all my soul for having inspired this longing in you. I do not doubt for one moment that it is your vocation, and I thank God for it from the bottom of my heart. . . . There is no vocation in the world as important as that of the priest—indeed, it is a thing not of this world, but of heaven. A priest is something *transcendent*, higher than anything else . . . What a vocation, my dear brother, and how I thank God for having given it you! There was a moment when I regretted not having been given it, regretted not having been invested with its sacred character. That was at the height of the Armenian persecution. Then I longed to be a priest, to know the language of these poor persecuted Christians, and be able to go from village to village, giving them heart to die for God. But I was not worthy of it.

But as for you—who can tell what God is reserving for you? The future is so obscure. God leads us by such unexpected paths. . . . If obedience ever takes you to those distant shores where so many souls are being lost for want of priests, where the harvest abounds but is being lost for want of laborers, give unending thanks to God. One is best off where one can do most good for others; to forget oneself completely in devoting oneself wholly to the children of our heavenly Father is to live the life of our Lord, the life of every Christian, and above all the true life of the priest. Moreover, if ever you are called to countries where nations sit in the shadow of death, then, too, give unending thanks to God, devoting yourself body and soul to making the light of Christ shine among souls sprinkled with his blood. It can be done in the

Trappist Order with wonderful results. Obedience will provide the means. . . .[20]

In his great joy Brother Marie-Albéric wrote a wonderful meditation on the Lord's Prayer on the evening of January 23.

Our Father

O God, how good you are to allow us to call you "our Father"! Who am I that my Creator, my King, my sovereign Master, should allow me to call him "Father"? And not only allows me to do so, but commands it. O God, how good you are! How frequently I should remind myself throughout my whole life of this most precious commandment. What gratitude, what joy, what love, and above all what confidence it should inspire in me. And as you are my Father and my God, how perfectly I should always hope in you. And again—as you are so good to me—how good I ought to be to others. It being your will to be my Father, Father to all men, I ought unfailingly to feel like a loving brother towards absolutely everyone, however wicked he may be.

I am filled with confusion, gratitude, trust and unshakeable hope, a filial love for God and a fraternal love for men.

Our Father, our Father, teach me to have your name continually on my lips with Jesus, in him and through him, for it is my greatest good fortune to be able to say it.

Our Father, our Father, may I live and die saying, "Our Father," and by my gratitude, love and obedience be truly your loyal son, a son pleasing to your heart. Amen.

Our Father, who art in heaven

Why did you choose this qualification rather than any other—

[20] From a letter dated January 24, 1897 (cf. OS, pp. 757–61; but taken here from the selection in B, pp. 143–5).

rather than "righteous Father," or "holy Father"? It was doubtless, O God, so that my soul might be uplifted from the very beginning of this prayer, lifted high above this poor world and placed from the outset where it ought always to be, both in this life and the next, in heaven, its native land. It was also to give us hope and peace from the first words of our prayers: Our Father is in heaven. How then, if we trust, should we not have hope and gentle peace?

It is also to put us from the outset in a state of joy, remembering that our Father, our God, our Beloved whom we love with all our hearts, all our souls, all our minds and all our strength, rejoices in infinite bliss for all eternity.

Hallowed be thy name

What is it, O Lord, that we are asking in these words? We are asking for the whole object of our desires, the whole aim and purpose of our lives, O Lord Jesus. We are asking for the revelation of the glory of God and the salvation of men through their thoughts, words and actions. For the revealing of your glory and the making perfect of men is one and the same thing.

Thus these words, "Hallowed be thy name" sum up the aim, at once both a single and a double aim, of all our prayers and the whole of our lives. With what love, what ardor we should sigh to you, O God, for the fulfilment of this petition!

How often our Lord said he had come into this world for the sole purpose of working for its fulfilment. How often he himself asked God for what he is telling us in these words to ask from him. This petition lay at the heart of all his prayers; it was the most fervent desire of his Heart, and its fulfilment was the goal of all his life's work.

May this petition also be the foundation of all our petitions, our prayers and longings; may we pray for God's glory and the salvation of men not merely when we say the *Pater*, but rather, in imitation of our Lord, may we make it the main object of all our prayers. May all our thoughts, words and actions have no other purpose than his.

Let us pray for it unceasingly, live for it alone—as our divine Exemplar did. May our aspirations, words and actions all lead to the sanctification of men, as our Lord's aspirations, words and actions all were directed to that end. This will not prevent us from praying and doing things with special intentions compatible with our general purpose—as our Lord prayed especially for the Apostles and taught or healed this particular individual or that. Our own insignificant acts will never have any visible influence except on individuals, yet we should still offer them to God, applying them to the general good and, in imitation of our Lord Jesus Christ, should always give first place in our prayers—prayers which reach up to and attain infinity—to this general petition for the revelation of God's glory and the salvation of the souls of men.

Thy Kingdom come

In this petition I am asking for exactly the same thing as in the last: the revelation of God's glory and the salvation of men. For what is the coming of the kingdom of God if it is not the acknowledgement of him as the only Master by everyone, to be obeyed from their hearts by all as their almighty and beloved king, everyone applying all his energies to serving his blessed king more perfectly—using his whole heart, mind, strength and soul in fulfilling to perfection God's least wishes? And what is such unparalleled zeal on the part of all men in serving the heavenly King with all their hearts but the revelation of God's glory and the salvation of mankind?

We should pray, aspire and guide all our activities towards this end. May our Lord teach us to make it not only the primary but also the secondary objective of our prayers. This petition should form the basis of our prayers, thoughts and desires, because our Lord inculcated it into us so strongly, and because we know that during his own lifetime it was the foundation of his prayer and converse with God.

Thy will be done on earth as it is in heaven

This petition is exactly the same as the two preceding ones. It asks for the same two things: the glory of God and the sanctification of men. What in fact are we asking when we pray that men may do God's will if not that they shall become saints? And it is precisely in the sanctity of men that the glorifying of God on earth consists.

Thus in this prayer taught me by our Lord, he wants me, before making any other request, to petition his Father three times for the revelation upon earth of his glory, and for the sanctification of men. That shows how close these two goals were to his heart, and how truly they were the foundation of his own sighs and prayers—just as they were also the whole purpose of his life in this world. It also shows me how much everything connected with the glorification of God and of value to souls rejoices our Lord's heart, since it is in conformity with his most fervent desires and with the whole of his life's work.

It shows me too to what extent every offense against God and everything that retards the sanctification of a soul is painful to his Heart, as being directly opposed to his most ardent desires, to those things he asked of the Father every day with tears and sighs, to those things for which he gave his blood. From this we can see how much those who, like blessed St. Teresa, endure heartbreak and extreme suffering at the sight or mention of the least sin committed by no matter whom, share the mind of the Lord. He himself tasted precisely the same sorrow in similar situations because he so ardently desired, so truly loved and so actively worked to give glory, praise and honor to his Father, and bring about the sanctification of men.

We also see how little they have in common with our Lord's mind who do not suffer to see sins committed or hear them described.

Inasmuch as one does not experience the vivid pain experienced by St. Teresa—and even more by our Lord—at every offense against God, one does not truly love the revelation of God's glory, and is very far from sharing the mind of Jesus. We should, therefore, find great joy in every good action, and long to perform it. We should have overwhelming zeal to do good, extraordinary pain and fear of doing anything offensive to God, and a great longing to avoid even the least sin. (It was in this spirit that our Lord drove the merchants from the Temple, and that St. John Chrysostom asked the faithful to reprove and even strike passers-by, the strangers whom they heard blaspheming.)

Give us this day our daily bread

What is it that we are asking here, O God? We are asking, both for today itself, and for the whole of this life (a life that in reality is no longer than a day) for that bread which is more precious than anything else—that is, our supernatural bread, the only bread we really need, the only bread absolutely necessary to us if we are to reach our goal: the necessary bread of grace.

There is, however, another supernatural bread which, without being absolutely indispensable like grace, is indispensable to many, and which is the best of all good things. The very word bread itself reminds us of it. It is that most precious good, that paramount good, the most holy Eucharist. One must notice, however, that in asking for these two kinds of bread, grace and the Eucharist, I do not ask for them for myself alone. I ask for "us," that is, for all men. I ask for nothing for myself alone. Everything I ask for in the *Pater* is either for God or for all mankind.

Forgetful of myself, thinking of myself only with my neighbor, of myself alone only in relation to God and to the same extent as I think of others—as behoves one who loves God above all things and his neighbor as himself—*that* is how the Lord wants me to be in all the petitions of the *Pater*. I should not pray for myself alone, but take great care to make my petitions on behalf of all men, for us all, our Lord's children whom he loves, for us all whom he has redeemed with his blood.

Forgive us our trespasses as we forgive

Having prayed to God that the goal of our Lord's life and our own may be attained, having asked him for what we need most if we are to attain it, asking it from him on behalf of all men, and having sighed with longing before him for the holy Eucharist, God himself, we now remind ourselves—having climbed so high—of what we really are. We remember the infinite lowliness of our souls which have such aspirations, desires and needs, and such a goal. And with this in mind, we say: Have mercy on us, for we are sinners.

With our whole souls, we ask God's forgiveness for ourselves and for all those who have offended God. We see how horrible our sins are, how horrible they are to God, how they disgust and insult him, how our Lord suffers in his Heart for each of the offenses committed against his Father. What sufferings he has prepared to undergo to expiate them and what a price he paid for them! And then, sharing our Lord's feelings, we humbly and penitently ask God's forgiveness. The pain of having offended him ourselves, and the pain of having seen him offended by so many others, issues from our hearts in the cry: Forgive us our trespasses. And, at the same time, realizing that one cannot seriously ask anyone for forgiveness if one does not oneself forgive, we perceive clearly that all the injuries which may have been done us are as nothing beside those we have done God, and we declare that we forgive them, that we disregard the evil that may have been done us, that we pay no attention to it, that we have forgotten it—and we beseech God for his part to forgive us our huge trespasses against him. We ask forgiveness, as we ask for grace, not for ourselves alone, but for all mankind.

Lead us not into temptation

Tell me, O Lord, what it is you would have me ask here, and why you should want it rather than something else? The petition is a cry suitable to every hour, every moment, of our lives—a cry for help. It is right that it should find its place in the *Pater,* for as we cannot help making it every minute of our lives, it should find its place in every prayer. I am so beset by enemies that not only is it impossible for me to attain my goal unless I call for help continually, but I cannot say anything at all, not even a short prayer, without crying for help.

Our Lord makes me say this prayer in the *Pater* because I continually need it, because it should be my soul's continual cry in every prayer, and because he would teach me to cry for help to him at any time.

Deliver us from evil

Deliver us from sin, the only real evil, the only evil that offends against you—this is evil to you. Deliver all men from sin, then they will all be saints and their sanctity will glorify you. Your glory will be revealed and their salvation assured, which is our whole desire. Deliver us then, O God, from evil, from sin, so that you may be glorified and men may be saved.

Like the first three petitions, this one also embraces everything we ought to ask, everything belonging to our goal, the purpose of the Church and of our Lord's life in this world. But it embraces all this in an indirect way, by turning our attention towards ourselves, asking for one of the things we need if we are to accomplish our purpose, while the first three clauses ask directly for our ultimate goal, the glory of God.[21]

Rome, January 23, 1897

[21] Cf. OS, pp. 585–93.

PART TWO

Nazareth
March 1897—August 1900

Leaving Brindisi on February 17, 1897, Charles de Foucauld reached Nazareth on March 5. On March 10, Mother St. Michael, Abbess of the Convent of the Poor Clares, took him in as a servant. He served the Poor Clares from that time onwards. When the sisters asked him, he frequently drew small holy pictures for them. In addition to these occupations, he used to pray before the Blessed Sacrament and write meditations in the little board hut where he lived.

"It is exactly the life I was looking for," he wrote to his cousin.[1]

After Brother Charles left the Trappists, the parish priest of St. Augustine, the Abbé Huvelin, once again became his director and wrote to him much more often than in earlier years.

In one of his meditations, Brother Charles has our Lord say:

"Look at the life I have fashioned for you: could it possibly parallel my hidden life more perfectly? You enjoy it in sum and in its least details. In the Trappist Order the resemblance was not close enough for you. But how perfectly it is now yours! How well I have treated you! You are living it at Nazareth, unknown, inordinately poor, lowly in your smock and sandals, a poor servant to poor nuns. Some take you for a laborer of the lowest kind; others think you are an outcast; some think you are perhaps the son of a criminal. Most—nearly all, in fact—take you for a fool.

---

[1] From a letter to Madame de Bondy, dated March 22, 1897 (cf. TPF, p. 101).

You obey the nuns and the portresses as I obeyed my parents. You give orders to nobody, absolutely no one. You work, doing what you are told sometimes by one person, sometimes by another, never doing anything for yourself, nothing you yourself choose to do. Your time is divided, as mine used to be, between work, prayer and sacred reading. It is split up as mine was, in just the way you think comes closest to my way of doing things, and in obedience to your director, who has given his approval of your division of it into prayer, reading and work. 'He that heareth him, heareth me.' [2] You are following me in all things by obeying my Father by always obeying your director, who tells you to do what I did, to be what I was, to live as I lived, to be a reflection of me in every way, in the place where you live, the life you lead, and above all in your soul." [3]

Between 1897 and 1900, Brother Charles wrote down the thoughts that came to him day by day in two small notebooks, headed Notes Spirituelles détachées (*Unconnected notes on the spiritual life*). *The following are a few extracts from them:*

Pentecost, June 6, 1897

O God, what is most displeasing to you in my soul? I lack the spirit of prayer, of confidence in you, love, meekness, loyalty and generosity. Jesus is not pleased with me. Dryness and darkness—everything is painful to me: Holy Communion, liturgical and mental prayer—everything, everything, even telling Jesus I love him. I must rivet myself to the life of faith. If I could only feel that Jesus loved me. But he never tells me so. What I principally lack is forgetfulness of myself and fraternal sympathy with others.

[2] Cf. Luke 10:16.
[3] From "Thoughts on the Feasts of Every Day of the Year," under date of June 17, 1898 (cf. NES, pp. 116 ff.).

(*Christ speaks:*) "You ask me how you have most offended me. By not loving me purely, wholeheartedly enough, by loving yourself and by loving created beings for your own sake and theirs. Do nothing for your own sake, nothing for creatures out of self-love, or love of them. In everything you have to do, have eyes only for me. In everything, ask yourself only what the Master would have done, and do that. Then you will love only me—then I shall live in you—you will lose yourself in me and live in me. There will be nothing of you left: my kingdom will have come in you.

✤

"*Your vocation:* Preach the Gospel silently as I did in my hidden life, and as also did Mary and Joseph.

"*Your rule:* Follow me. Do what I did. In every situation ask yourself: What would our Lord have done? Then do that. That is your only rule, but it is absolutely binding on you.

"*Your mind:* It should be full of the love of God, forgetful of yourself. It should be full of the contemplation and joy of my beatitude, of compassion and sorrow for my sufferings, and of joy at my joys. It should be full of suffering for the sins committed against me and an ardent longing to glorify me. It should be a mind full of love for your neighbor for my sake, for I love all men as a father loves his children. It should be full of longing for the spiritual and material good of all men for my sake. It should be a mind free, tranquil, at peace. Everything in it should be there for God's sake alone; nothing for your own sake, or for the sake of any creature.

"Your interior prayer: First method: 1. What do you want to say to me, O God? 2. For my own part, this is what I want to tell you— 3. Saying nothing else, gaze on the Beloved.— Second Method: *Quis? Quid? Ubi? Quibus auxiliis? Cur? Quomodo? Quando?* [4]

"Attendance at Mass: Divide it into three parts: 1. Up to the consecration: offer me and offer yourself to my Father and bring your intentions before him. Give thanks to me for my cross, asking my forgiveness for having made it necessary. 2. From the consecration to the Communion: adore me on the altar. 3. After the Communion: adore me in your heart, give thanks to me, love me, rejoice, be silent.

"Thinking about death: Remember that you ought to die as a martyr, stripped of everything, stretched naked on the ground, unrecognizable, covered with wounds and blood, killed violently and painfully—and desire that it be today. That I may grant you this infinite grace, watch loyally, carry your cross faithfully. Remember that your death must inevitably flow out of your life— and on that account, realize the insignificance of a great many things. Think often of death, so as to prepare for it and appraise things at their true value." [5]

*

I do not ask Jesus for consolations (primarily because I do not deserve them), because if he granted them it would be such joy

[4] A very ancient method of meditation on the Scriptures: Who took part in the incident? What did they do? Where was it? Who else was present? Why? In what way did things happen? When?

[5] Charles de Foucauld wrote these words in 1897. Nineteen years later, on December 1, 1916, he was murdered by Sennousis at Tamanrasset.

to hear him, to feel him deep in my heart, that I should be in paradise, and we cannot have our paradise both in this world and in the next. I ask only one thing of him: that I may be loyal to him. But alas, my loyalty is so weak.

It is right that a soul so lacking in fervor should never taste bliss. God sometimes allows us to be in such profound darkness that not a single star shines in our skies. The reason is that we must be reminded that we are on earth only to suffer, while following our gentle Saviour along a dark and thorny path. We are pilgrims and strangers on earth. Pilgrims sleep in tents and sometimes cross deserts, but the thought of their homeland makes them forget everything else. Yes, on earth we are indeed in an alien world—we ought to hang up our harps and weep.[6]

In absolutely every situation my only desire is to fulfil the divine will. But alas, I have so little love for Jesus that I dare not call him my Beloved. Yet I want—I long—to love him more than anything on earth or in heaven. My heart and my life are his alone.

When you feel tired, sad, lonely, a prey to suffering, withdraw into the intimate sanctuary of your soul, and there you will find your *brother*, your *friend Jesus*, who will be your consolation, your stay and your strength.

(*Jesus speaks, answering him:*) "Putting it all in a single phrase, my child: abandon everything, and you will find all things."

*

O how fortunate I am now in my beloved solitude, far, very far, from this world where so many offenses are committed against him. How blessed we are when we are alone with his love, alone with his tenderness! I do not feel so great a love, yet he knows

[6] Cf. Psalm 136:1–2.

that I love him more than the whole world. Completely worthless as I am, my heart, my soul, my whole life are all his till my last breath. Alas, I do not love him, at least not as I should. Words are nothing: we must show it in actions. Ask that my love may be generous, loyal, ardent!

*

Since the sin of Adam, man has been able to do nothing good on earth in either the material or spiritual order, without an effort at least proportionate to that good. Good in the spiritual order being infinitely superior and the love of God being the highest good, *they can be purchased only at the price of endeavors reaching the intensity of pain,* of sufferings that become the more poignant the higher the good we are striving to attain. *The interior darkness and sufferings the soul experiences in its interior life in the divine love are alone sufficiently excruciating to serve as the price—the cash price, dare I say?—of purchasing the highest good, the divine love.* That is why the only condition on which we can begin to love God is that we should *buy* our love with interior darkness and sufferings *proportionate to* the level of love we are going to achieve.

*

How greatly we should long for all men to be in a state of grace! In other words, we should long to see as many living tabernacles, as many bodies and souls animated by Jesus, as there are souls in the world. How greatly we should long to see souls in a state of grace doing the holiest of all possible actions! In other words, we should long to see the reduplication of all the acts of Jesus, for each of them gives infinite glory to God.[7]

[7] Cf. ES, pp. 170–6.

In his meditations on the Psalms, he wrote in 1898, on Psalm 1:

You tell me I shall be happy, filled with the happiness of true blessedness, on the last day—that even in my present wretchedness, I am a palm tree planted beside living waters, the living waters of God's will, love and grace—and that I shall bring forth fruit in its proper season. You take the trouble to console me; I feel I am without fruit, without good works. I tell myself: it is eleven years since I was converted, and what have I done? What are my good works beside those of the saints? I see myself with hands empty of anything good. You take the trouble to console me, saying: You will bear your fruit in *your* proper season. But what season is that? The proper season for us all is the day of judgment. You promise that poor as I am if I persevere in the good fight with a good will I shall bear fruit at that last hour.

And you add: you will be a fine tree with leaves eternally green, and all your works will prosper in the end; they will all bear fruit in eternity. O God, how good you are! How divinely consoling is the Heart of Jesus! It is as though you had dictated these first words in the Book of Psalms to tell us what you once said by the Sea of Galilee: "My yoke is sweet and my burden light." [8] I thank you, my God, for the consolation you give us, consolation of which our hearts stand in such great need. [9]

Brother Charles was at Nazareth the servant of the Poor Clares. He spent his time praying and humbling himself with Jesus of Nazareth.

Nazareth, September 30, 1897

All we are trying to do is be one with Jesus, to reproduce his

[8] Matt. 11:30.
[9] Meditations on the Psalms and Prophets (cf. OS, p. 795).

life in our own, to proclaim his teaching from the rooftops in our thoughts, words and actions, to let him rule and live in us. He comes into us so frequently in the Holy Eucharist—may he establish his kingdom within us! If he gives us joys, we should accept them gratefully: the Good Shepherd gives us such sweet grasses to strengthen us and make us fit to follow him later along dry pathways. If he gives us crosses, we should embrace them: *bona crux*.[10] To be given a cross is the best grace of all: it is to walk hand in hand with Jesus more closely than ever, to relieve him by carrying his cross for him, as Simon of Cyrene did. It is our Beloved's invitation to us to declare and prove our love for him. In torments of soul and bodily suffering, "let us rejoice and be glad"; Jesus is calling us, telling us to tell him we love him, and to go on telling him as long as our suffering lasts.

Every cross, great or small, every discomfort even, is an appeal from our Beloved, asking us to declare our love and go on doing so while the cross lasts. When we think of it like this, could we not wish that our cross could last for ever? It will last as long as Jesus wishes. However sweet it may be, however greatly loved, we desire it only as long as it is Jesus' will for us. Your will, not ours, Brother Jesus. As for ourselves, we should think no more of ourselves than as if we did not exist. We should think only of you, our beloved Spouse. We want not what seems good to us, but what is good to you. We ask nothing for ourselves; all we ask is your glory. "Hallowed be thy name: thy kingdom come: thy will be done" in your children, in all men. May these things be done in us. May we give all possible glory to you throughout our lives. May we do your will—may we give all possible solace to your Heart. That is all we want and all we need. We are here at your feet, do with us as you will—whatever it may be, do it ac-

[10] Good Cross.

cording to your will. We have no will, no wish except to fulfil
your will, to do what seems good to you.[11]

*At the beginning of November 1897, Brother Charles made a
long retreat. During it he burst out with joy at being in Nazareth
at last and at the vocation God had given him. At the end of the
retreat, he wrote down a certain number of resolutions.*

1. To embrace humility, poverty, abandonment, humiliation,
solitude and suffering with Jesus in the manger; to reckon as
nothing human greatness, the respect and esteem of men, and to
give equal honor to the poorest man as to the richest. For myself,
to seek always the very lowest place, so arranging my life as to be
the least of all, the most despised of men.

When I am heavy-hearted, discouraged with myself, or by other
people or things, I will recall the glory of Jesus, who sits for all
time at the right hand of God, and I will rejoice. At these times, I
will also say the Glorious Mysteries of the Rosary, so as to be
bathed in joy.

(Jesus Christ speaks:) "Generally, do not be disturbed by little
things. Throw all little matters aside and try to live at a very high
level, not from pride, but from love.

"Cast aside everything but me. Make a desert here where you
can be alone with me—as Mary Magdalene was alone in the
desert with me. You will reach this goal by detachment, by expelling from your mind all those small concerns, those infinitely
little things which, though not evil in themselves, would in the end
take your mind away from me from morning till night, when it
should be contemplating me from morning till night.

"Pay attention to me when you are working for me, and when

---

[11] From a letter to Father Jerome (cf. ES, pp. 178–9).

you are praying. Pay unceasing attention to me, and devote as long as possible to interior prayer and sacred reading, for they will make you one with me and through them I shall speak to you as I used to speak to my parents and Mary Magdalene at Nazareth and Bethany. When one loves something, one looks at it continually, reckoning as well employed all the time devoted to contemplating it and as lost all the time it is out of sight. The only time that seems important is the time spent looking at this one thing which to our eyes then is the only thing that seems to exist. Everything else is emptiness and nothingness to us. Base yourself on me. Lose yourself in me, immerse yourself in my love. Think of the time I have told you to long for, when you will lean eternally on my breast. . . ."

Never miss a possible moment, an instant, in the presence of the Blessed Sacrament, whatever the moral or physical difficulties may be, or the suffering or danger of giving offense involved in being there. The whole universe is nothing beside the Master of the universe who dwells in the tabernacle.

Be humble in thought, word and action.

Neither seek nor approve the respect of men, but rejoice in their scorn.

When one is in love, one is humble, one sees oneself as very insignificant, as nothing beside one's beloved.

When one loves, one imitates one's beloved—and Jesus was meek and humble of heart.

Humility is the crown of all the virtues and a necessity to those who would be pleasing to God. Pride negates them all.

Should I cling to being at Nazareth? No, no more than to anything else. Cling to nothing but the will of God, but God alone. It ought to be a great blessing to me to live at Nazareth; I must reckon it a great blessing and be very grateful for it, but not become attached to it. As soon as it ceases to be God's will, I shall have to go immediately, without a backward glance, to wherever his will calls me.

(*Our Lord speaks:*) "One of the reasons why I wanted to be poorer than the poorest worker was because I came to teach men to despise honors, to despise this world's goods, and because I wanted to give them an example of the most extreme poverty and the most profound abasement. Do the same thing. Your reasons will be the same as mine, with one last one: it is part of your vocation to proclaim the Gospel from the rooftops, not by what you say, but by how you live."

How can I repay God what I owe him when I have received so much? By love. By obedience to his will for me in all things— for obedience is the sign of love. By doing my duties perfectly, which is connected with perfect obedience. And especially by doing two things which in the degree in which I am bound to offer them are matters of counsel, not precept, special labors of love, expressive of the heart's tenderness and ardor. These two things are being fervent in the prayers that make up my daily bouquet of roses, and doing penance—which is a sacrifice, a gift, a daily little Calvary, the perfume of myrrh I offer daily for the embalming of my Beloved. Prayer and peace should be the basis of my life, as they were of the life of Jesus of Nazareth and of St. Mary Magdalene in Sainte Baume.[12]

I should not rejoice for my own sake when my physical sufferings are relieved. I should welcome relief for God's sake, for his sake alone, because it is his will—not for my own personal pleasure. When the will of God is not made obvious, my personal preference should be for penance, because it offers a greater sacrifice to God. But above all, I should wish to see the will of

---

[12] The "holy cave" in Provence where St. Mary Magdalene is traditionally said to have ended her life in meditation and prayer—see below, p. 65, n. 17.

God fulfilled, because the fulfillment of his will is what honors him most of all.

The desire to offer the biggest possible sacrifice to God should be neither a constraint nor a source of sadness to me. I should possess the sacred freedom of the sons of God, crying continually *Abba: Father,* and rejoice in God. I should not be held back by the instinctive fear the devil always inspires in us at the beginning of any good work—"he works through fear"—and, by making us afraid, seeks to deter us from everything good, especially penance. "God loves a cheerful giver." [13]

On retreat at Ephrem—a place near the desert to which Jesus withdrew with his apostles shortly before his death to prepare himself and them for his passion—Brother Charles meditated on the Beatitudes.

(*Jesus speaks:*)

"Blessed are the poor in spirit—those who reject not only material things, which is the first step, but who also climb higher, emptying their souls completely of every attachment, every liking, every desire, every search of which I am not the object. Such poverty of spirit leaves the soul completely empty, voiding it of love for material things, for one's neighbor and for oneself, expelling everything, absolutely everything, from it, leaving it a completely empty space which can be filled wholly by me. Then I can make divine the love for material things they have expelled from their souls so as to give all the room in them to me. They have expelled all these different loves from their souls, and I occupy them completely, so that they are empty of everything else and full of me. Then, in me and for my sake, they begin to love all

[13] From Retreat at Nazareth (cf. ES, pp. 118–22).

these other things again, no longer for the sake of the things themselves, but for mine. Then shall their charity[14] be ordered aright. They love all created things for my sake, loving nothing for its own sake, because they owe all their love to me and should lose themselves in me, possessing nothing, not even love, except through me or for my sake. Blessed are the poor in spirit, who are empty of everything else, but so full of me!

"Blessed are they that hunger—those who hunger for justice, the rule of justice on earth, for my reign on earth, who hunger to see me glorified by every soul, who hunger to see my will perfectly fulfilled by all creatures. You should never be without this great hunger for justice, for seeing my will perfectly fulfilled by both yourself and all mankind, for your own total sanctification and the perfect sanctity of all men. This is the hunger that weighs on my own Heart. Feel it more and more, not for your own sake, or for man's, but for God's sake, for the love of God. You will then be blessed indeed, for you will be in perfect harmony with my own heart.

"Blessed are they that mourn—because they are unhappy, poor, bereaved, sick, suffering in body or soul, tried in whatever way. They are blessed because their sufferings will be effective in expiating their sins, because their sufferings detach them from the world and lift up their gaze to me and attach them to myself. More blessed still are those who mourn their sins. And yet more blessed those who weep for sorrow at not seeing me and at being exiled far from me in this vale of tears. Even more blessed are those who mourn my sufferings, my passion, all the sufferings I endured on earth. And most blessed are those who weep from love alone, who weep because they love me, who weep for no particular

[14] Charity: the theological virtue of love of God and of neighbor.

reason—not from pain nor yet longing, but merely because when they think of me their whole heart melts and they cannot restrain their tears.

"Blessed are they that are hated and persecuted for my sake—blessed indeed for they are imitating me, sharing my lot. True spouses, they share fully in the lot of their Spouse. Blessed, because is there anything more loving than to suffer with the one you love? Blessed, because they have this double happiness, suffering with their Beloved and for him. Blessed, because through these very sufferings their love for me will grow, increasing proportionately to their sufferings for my sake—and their growing love will not be transitory, but enduring: it will last through time and into eternity. O blessed are they who suffer persecution with me, whose love is growing continually under persecution! Never reject or fear pains, hatred and persecution suffered for my sake; on the contrary, accept them with joy, blessing, thanksgiving, gratitude to God and men, thanking me from the bottom of your heart, praying for your enemies and executioners, joining—terrestrial angels —with the holy guardian angels in begging me for their conversion, rejoicing from the depths of your hearts at having been found worthy to undergo suffering and humiliation for love of me. Never forget that this is how I treat all those I love especially fondly. . . .

"And how blessed the end of these sufferings will be! The more you have loved me and suffered for me in this world, the more you have been persecuted for my sake, the clearer will be your vision of me, and the more perfectly you will love me for ever in the next."

At five o'clock in the afternoon: Speak, Lord, for thy servant heareth. . . .

"Love your enemies, do good to them that hate you. Bless them that curse you. . . . To him that striketh thee on the one cheek, offer also the other. And him that taketh away from thee thy cloak, forbid him not to take thy coat also. Give to everyone that asketh thee; and of him that taketh away thy goods, ask them not again. . . . And as you would that men should do to you, do you also to them. . . . Be merciful . . . Judge not, and you shall not be judged. . . . Forgive, and you shall be forgiven. . . . Why seest thou the mote in thy brother's eye, but the beam that is in thy own eye thou considerest not? [15]

"All these commandments, my children, are the precepts of charity and you would not find them surprising if you could once and for all really grasp that all human beings together make up a single family, whose common Father, Creator and Preserver is God, who is Father to all men equally. He loves all human beings incomparably more than the most loving father loves his children. It is his will that concord, love and tenderness should reign among his sons and faithful people, who are all, without exception, so greatly loved themselves. To these dispositions should be united, when necessary, that indulgence and fondness which are always ready to yield, and which any loving father likes to see reign among his children. It is his will, therefore, that they should yield freely to one another, each giving up his rights and never thinking of reclaiming them. They should yield to the unjust brother, so as to correct him gently and keep peace in the family, only praying for him so that he may correct himself.

"Finally, notice that the only aim of the whole of this list of my recommendations to you is the maintenance of peace and love among all the brethren making up the great family of mankind. Keep all these commandments, and carve deeply into the founda-

[15] Cf. Luke 6:27–41.

tions of your soul the chief commandment from which all the others spring: all human beings are really and truly *brothers* in God, their common Father, and it is God's will that they should look on one another, love one another and treat one another in every way as the fondest of brothers.

"And be compassionate with one another: look how compassionate I am to you, how I suffer, how I take pity and compassion on every sorrow, how I sigh with this one, and weep with that. I have compassion on their mourning, their sicknesses, their troubles, their hunger, weaknesses and ignorance. Not only do I do good to both souls and bodies, but I have pity in my Heart, profound compassion for all the ills of souls and bodies. There is a place for compassion in the love of every human heart and in all human love." [16]

While at Nazareth, Brother Charles wrote many meditations on the Gospels as an aid to prayer. He used small notebooks, filling them with his fine handwriting in the course of nights and days spent in prayer before the most Blessed Sacrament. The following are some extracts from these meditations.

POVERTY

O my Lord Jesus, here is your divine poverty. How greatly I need your direction—you loved poverty so much. Already in the Old Testament you showed your predilection for it. During your life on earth you made it your faithful companion. You left it as an inheritance to your saints, to all those ready to follow you, to all those who would be your disciples. You inculcated it by the example of your whole life and glorified it, beatified it, and de-

---

[16] "Eight Days in Ephrem," March 1898 (cf. ES, pp. 144–9).

clared the necessity of it in your preaching. You chose poor laborers to be your parents. You were born in a cave used as a stable. You worked in poverty during your childhood. Your first worshipers were shepherds. When you were presented in the Temple, the offering made for you was the offering of the poor. You lived as a poor working man for thirty years in Nazareth, where I am fortunate enough to live, where I have the immeasurable, profound, inexpressible joy, the bliss of raking dung into heaps. Then, during your public life, you lived on alms among poor fishermen you had chosen to be your companions. "Without a stone to put under your head." As you told St. Teresa, at that time you frequently slept in the open air, for lack of a roof to shelter under. On Calvary you were stripped of your clothes, your only possession, and soldiers gambled for them among themselves. You died naked, and you were buried by charity and by strangers. "Blessed are the poor!"

My Lord Jesus, how quickly he makes himself poor who, loving you with all his heart, will not permit himself to be richer than his Beloved. My Lord Jesus, how quickly he becomes poor who, remembering that whatever is done for one of your little ones is done for you and whatever is not done for them is not done for you, relieves all the sufferers who come to his gate. How quickly he becomes poor who accepts *with faith your words:* "If you would be perfect, sell all you have and give it to the poor . . . Blessed are the poor, for whoever shall have given up his possessions for my sake, shall receive them back a hundredfold here below, and in heaven shall have eternal life," and so many others like them.

My God, I do not know how it is possible for some souls to see you in poverty and themselves voluntarily remain rich, to imagine themselves so much grander than their Master, their Beloved, and not want to be like him in all things—as far as it is for them to decide—and especially in your humbleness. I do not doubt their love for you, my God, but I think there is something lacking in their love—I, at any rate, could not imagine love without a *longing*, a *compelling longing*, to imitate, to resemble the Beloved, and especially to share all his life's pains, difficulties and burdens. To be rich, to live in comfort among my possessions while you were poor, deprived, living in misery under the burden of heavy labor—I just could not do it, O God. I could not love like that. "The servant is not above his master," neither is the bride rich while the Bridegroom is poor—especially when he is voluntarily poor, and perfect as well. St. Teresa, tired of the pressures put on her to accept an income for her convent at Avila, sometimes came close to accepting, but when she returned to her oratory and saw the cross, she fell at its feet and begged Jesus, naked on his cross, to give her the grace never to accept an income and to be as poor as he was. I am judging no one, O God; the others are your servants and my brothers, and I cannot but love them, do good to them, pray for them. But for my own part I cannot understand love that does not seek to imitate and does not feel the need to share every cross.

Besides, the poor man's possessions are so great: he has nothing and loves nothing in this world, and so his soul is free. Nothing is especially important to him. It is of little significance to him whether he is sent to one place or another, for he has nothing anywhere, and wants nothing anywhere. He finds God everywhere, and God is the only one from whom he wants anything. Moreover, if he is loyal, God always gives him what is best for his soul. How free he is! How lightly his spirit mounts up into the heavens! How weightless are his wings! His prayers are little troubled by thoughts of natural things great or small (for little things, even the smallest, are as disturbing as the biggest): how little they distract his prayers! Such things do not exist for him.

This was the point you, blessed Mary Magdalene, had reached

at Sainte Baume.[17] And I believe Jesus has given me you to teach me poverty, complete, perfect poverty, not merely "having no more than, and being able to call on no more than, the poorest worker" as I vowed, and as the imitation of Jesus requires. Total poverty is more than this. It is *poverty of Spirit* which you, Lord Jesus, said was blessed, that makes every—absolutely every—material thing a matter of complete indifference, so that we can brush everything aside, break with everything as St. Mary Magdalene did in the holy cave. This is the poverty that leaves no attachments at all to temporal things, but completely empties the heart, leaving it whole and entirely free for God alone. God then refills it with himself, reigning in it alone, filling it wholly with himself, and putting into it—though not for itself, but for himself, for his own sake—love for all men, his children.

The heart then knows nothing and holds nothing but these two loves. Nothing else exists for it any longer, and it lives on earth as though it were not there, and in continuous contemplation of the only real necessity, the *only Being*, and in intercession for those whom the Heart of God longs to love.[18]

LOWLINESS

O my Lord Jesus, graciously permit me to be you in this meditation. It was you who said: "The servant is not above his master," and in doing so you commanded me not to be higher than you

[17] Charles de Foucauld had taken Mary Magdalene (traditionally identified with the sinner and the sister of Lazarus) as his special spiritual mother. According to a French tradition of great antiquity, after the first persecution of Christians in Palestine (cf. Acts 8:1–4), Mary Magdalene went to Provence with other refugee Christians and lived there for many years as an anchoress in "Sainte Baume"—the holy cave—devoting herself to the love of the Lord and to prayer. She is one of the patron saints of France.

[18] From Retreat at Nazareth, November 1897 (cf. ES, pp. 104–8).

in the eyes of men, as far as my life in this world is concerned. How ought I to practise this lowliness?

(*Jesus answers:*) "Notice first that after I said 'the servant is not above his master' I added, 'it is enough for the servant if he be as his master.' Thus I do not want you to be above me, but no more do I want you to be lower than me. If there are exceptions to this, there is certainly none for you, whom I have so often called to the vocation of imitating me perfectly and me alone. Try then to be in the eyes of the world what I was during my life at Nazareth, neither higher nor lower. I was a poor working man, living by the labor of my hands: men took me for unlearned, illiterate. As my parents, near relatives, cousins and friends I chose poor laborers like myself, artisans and fishermen. I spoke to them on equal terms; I dressed like them, lived like them and ate like them while I was with them. Like all poor people, I was exposed to scorn, and it was because in the eyes of the world I was a poor 'Nazarene' that I was so persecuted and ill-treated during my public ministry—that the first time I spoke in the synagogue at Nazareth they wanted to throw me down a cliff, while in Galilee they called me Beelzebub and in Judaea devil and possessed. It was why they treated me as an impostor and traitor and killed me on a gallows between two thieves. They took me for an ambitious nobody.

"Be taken as what I was taken for, my child, unlearned, poor, of lowly birth, also for what you really are: unintelligent, untalented and ungifted. Always look for the meanest tasks, but cultivate your mind as far as your director bids. But do it secretly. Do not let the world know. I was infinitely wise, but no one knew it. Do not be afraid to study; it is good for your soul. Study zealously to become better, to know me and love me better, to know my will and do it more perfectly, and also to become more like me, who am perfect Knowledge. Be very unlearned in the eyes of men, and very learned in the knowledge of God at the foot of my tabernacle. I was lowly and despised beyond all measure.

"Seek out, ask for and love those occupations that will humiliate you: piling dung, digging, whatever is lowest and most uncouth. The less important you are in this way, the more like me you will be. If you are thought a fool, so much the better. Give infinite thanks for it to me. They treated me as a madman—it is one of the ways I offer you of being like me. If they throw stones at you, mock you, curse you in the streets, so much the better. Thank me for it: I am giving you an infinite grace—for did they not do as much for me? How fortunate you should think yourself when I give you such close resemblance to me. But do not do anything to merit such treatment—nothing eccentric or strange. I did nothing so as to be treated like that: I did not deserve it—on the contrary. But still they did it to me. Equally, you must do nothing to deserve it, but if I give you the grace of being subjected to it, thank me generously. Do nothing to hinder it, and do not stop it. Endure everything with great joy and gratitude to the Lord that gives it, as though it were a most acceptable present from a brother.

"Do everything as I would have done it and everything I did. Do not do only pleasant things, but devote yourself to the meanest tasks. In everything—your dress, your lodging, the freedom and politeness of your manner to the unimportant—show your level to be that of the lowest. Carefully hide anything that might raise you in your neighbor's eyes. But in my presence, in the silence and solitude of the tabernacle, study and read, for then you are alone with me, my holy parents and your mother St. Mary Magdalene, and the doors are shut. At my feet, you should expand, doing whatever your director tells you to improve yourself and make yourself more holy—so as to bring greater consolation to my heart." [19]

[19] From Retreat at Nazareth, November 1897 (cf. ES, pp. 108–11).

MANUAL LABOR

O God, inspire me with the knowledge you want me to have regarding manual work.

"In this matter, as in lowliness and poverty, I want from you what I required from myself. Yours is a blessed vocation, my child—how fortunate you are! Just take me as a model: do what you think I did and what I would have done. Do not do what you think I should not have done or would not do. Imitate me.

"Work hard enough to earn your daily bread, but less than ordinary workers. They work to earn as much as possible. You and I work only so as to earn a very frugal diet and the poorest of clothing and lodgings, together with enough to give small sums in alms. We do not work more than this, because our detachment from material things and our love of penance lead us to want only the poorest possible clothing, lodging and food, and only what is absolutely necessary. We work less than other workers because on the one hand we have fewer material needs, and on the other we have greater spiritual needs. We try and keep more time for prayer, mental prayer and spiritual reading, because that is what life was like in the holy house at Nazareth."

How should I work?

"In constant recollection of me, my child, remembering continually that you are working with me and for me, that I myself, Mary and Joseph, St. Mary Magdalene and our angels are with you; with them, you should contemplate me continually." [20]

FAITH

> *"Why are ye fearful,*
> *O ye of little faith?"*
> Matt. 8:26

[20] From Retreat at Nazareth (cf. ES, pp. 111–12).

Complete freedom from fear is one of those things we owe wholly to our Lord. To be afraid is to do him a double injury. First, it is to forget him, to forget that he is with us, that he loves us and is himself almighty, and second it is to fail to bend to his will. If we shape our will to his, as everything that happens is either willed or allowed by him, we shall find joy in whatever happens, and shall never be disturbed or afraid.

So then, we should have the faith that banishes all fear. Beside us, face to face with us, within us, we have our Lord Jesus, our God whose love for us is infinite, who is himself almighty, who has told us to seek for the kingdom of God and that everything else will be given us. In that blessed and omnipotent company, we must go straight along the path of the greatest perfection, certain that nothing will happen to us that we cannot use as a source of the greatest good for his glory and the sanctification of ourselves and others, and that everything that happens is either willed or permitted by him, and that therefore, far from lying under the shadow of fear, we have only to say, "Whatever happens—God be praised!" praying that he will arrange everything not in accordance with our ideas, but for his greater glory. We should never forget the two axioms: "Jesus is with me.—Whatever happens, happens by the will of God."

> *"Be of good heart, my daughter;*
> *thy faith hath made thee whole"*
> Matt. 9:22

Faith is the virtue most commonly rewarded and praised by our Lord. Sometimes, as in the case of St. Mary Magdalene, he praised love, at others, humility. But such cases are rare. Almost always it was faith he rewarded and praised.

Why was this? Doubtless because although faith is not the highest virtue (charity surpasses it), it is nonetheless the most important, both because it is the foundation of all the others, including charity, and because it is the most rare. How wonderful it is really to have the faith which inspires the believer's every action. Such faith is supernatural, and strips the mask from the world and reveals God in everything. It makes nothing impossible; it renders meaningless such words as anxiety, danger and fear, so that the believer goes through life calmly and peacefully, with profound joy—like a child hand in hand with his mother. It fixes the soul in an attitude of such complete detachment from all material things that it can clearly perceive their nothingness and puerility. It gives to prayer the confidence a child shows in asking its father for something reasonable. It shows the believer that "apart from doing something pleasing to God, there is nothing that is not a lie." It puts everything in a new light, revealing men as images of God, to be loved and venerated as portraits of our Beloved, and to be made the recipients of all possible good, and showing us that every other created thing without exception is there to be used as an aid in getting to heaven, by praising God through it, either by our actively using it or by our definite rejection of it.

It is this faith which, by letting us perceive the splendor of God, lets us see our littleness. It leads us to undertake everything pleasing to God, without hesitation, or self-consciousness, never fearing and never drawing back. What a rare thing such faith is. O God, give it to me! I believe—but make my faith grow. O God, I beseech you in the name of our Lord Jesus Christ: give me faith and love. Amen.

> *"O thou of little faith,*
> *why didst thou doubt?"*
> Matt. 14:31

What great faith our Lord Jesus Christ asks of us—and how just that is. Do we not owe him such faith? After our Lord had said, "Come," St. Peter should no longer have been afraid, but should have walked confidently on the water. And in the same way, when it is clear that Jesus has called us to a particular position, has given us a vocation, we should fear nothing, but should approach the most insurmountable obstacles fearlessly. Jesus has said, "Come": we have been given the grace to walk on the waves. It looks impossible to us, but Jesus is Master of the impossible. What we have to do is three things:

First, we must do as Peter did: ask our Lord to call us quite clearly to him. Then, having distinctly heard his "Come," we should throw ourselves unhesitatingly into the water, as St. Peter did. Without it, we have no right to throw ourselves into the water, for that would be presumption and imprudence, a grave imperiling of our lives; it would be a sin, and often by its results a grave sin, for to endanger the life of the soul is even more criminal than to risk the life of the body. Until we hear his "Come," our duty is to watch and pray. Then, lastly, trusting God's "Come," we must walk on the waves till the end, without a shadow of anxiety, certain —by virtue of that word "Come"—that if we walk faithfully and loyally, everything along the path Jesus calls us to follow will be made smooth for us. So then, let us walk with absolute faith in the path along which he is calling us, for heaven and earth will pass away, but his word will not.[21]

HOPE

O God, tell me about hope! How can hopeful thoughts originate in this poor world? Are they not bound to come from heaven? Everything we see, all we experience, all we are only proves our nothingness to us. How can we realize we were created to be Jesus' brothers and co-heirs, and your children, unless you tell

[21] From "Meditations on Gospel Texts on the Principal Virtues" (cf. ES, pp. 37–40).

us so? Mother of Beautiful Love and Sacred Hope, pray to your Son Jesus for me and inspire in me the thoughts I should have.

The hope of being one day in heaven, at your feet, my Lord, in the company of the holy Virgin and the saints, gazing on you, loving you, possessing you for all eternity, with nothing able ever to separate me from you for a single moment, my Good and my All—what a vision that is! A vision of true peace, of heavenly peace indeed. It is a hope far above our dreams and raises us far above our normal selves. Yet you not only permit us to have it, you tell us we must have it. Could you possibly have given us a pleasanter commandment? O God, how good you are!

Hope is symbolized by an anchor—and how secure that anchor is! However wicked I may be, however great a sinner, I *must* hope that I shall go to heaven. You *forbid* me to despair. However ungrateful or lukewarm or cowardly I may be, however much I may misuse your graces, O God, you make it my *duty* to hope to live eternally at your feet in love and holiness. You forbid me ever to be discouraged by my shortcomings, or to say to myself, "I can go no further. The road is too bad. I must go back—right back to the bottom." You forbid me to say to myself at the prospect of the sins I renew daily, the sins I ask you daily to forgive and continually fall back into: "I can never correct myself; holiness is not for me; heaven and I have nothing in common and I am too unworthy to go there." Even when I think of the infinite graces you have heaped on me and the unworthiness of my present life, you *forbid* me to say to myself, "I have gone too far in misusing my graces; I ought to be a saint, but I am a sinner; I cannot correct myself, it is too difficult; I am nothing but wretchedness and pride; after everything God has done, there is still no good in me; I shall never go to heaven."

In spite of everything, you want me to hope, to hope always that I shall receive enough grace to be converted and attain glory.

What is there in common between heaven and me—between its perfection and my wretchedness? There is your Heart, O Lord Jesus. It forms a link between these two so dissimilar things. There is the love of the Father who so loved the world he gave his only Son. I *must* always hope, because you have commanded me to, and because I *must* always believe both in your love, the love you have so firmly promised, and in your power. Yes indeed, remembering what you have done for me, I must always have such confidence in your love that, however ungrateful and unworthy I may seem to myself to be, I can still have hope in it, still count on it, still remain convinced that you are ready to accept me as the father accepted his prodigal son—and even more ready—and still remain convinced too that you will not stop calling me to your feet, inviting me to come to them and giving me the means to do so.[22]

PRAYER

(Jesus speaks:)

"When you pray, you should want all that I want, and only what I want, in the way I want it, and to the extent I want it: 'Father, may your will be done!' This is the prayer you will say forever in heaven.

"Everything God desires, and consequently, everything you desire, everything God wills, and consequently, everything you want, are to be found in the words: 'Father, may your will be done.'

"Prayer is any converse between the soul and God. Hence it is that' state in which the soul looks wordlessly on God, solely occupied with contemplating him, telling him with looks that it loves him, while uttering no words, even in thought.

[22] From Retreat at Nazareth (cf. ES, pp. 91–3).

"*The best prayer is that in which there is the most love.* The more heavily the soul's glances are charged with love, the more tenderly, the more lovingly, the soul behaves in the presence of God, the more perfect its love is. Prayer in the widest sense of the word can be either silent contemplation or contemplation accompanied by words—words of adoration, or love, or self-oblation, the giving to God of everything that is in one. They can be words of thanksgiving for the goodness of God, or for favors granted to oneself or other created beings. They may be words of apology in reparation for one's own sins or those of another; they may convey a petition.

"*My children: in prayer, do what I would have you do—love, love, love.*

"Besides the time you should devote every day solely to prayer, you should lift up your soul towards me as often as possible throughout the rest of the day. Depending on the nature of your work you may be able to do so by thinking continually of me (as is possible in certain manual occupations), or you may only be able to lift up your eyes towards me from time to time. At least, let it be as frequently as possible. It would be very wonderful and very right to be able to contemplate me unceasingly, never losing sight of me. But in this world that is not possible for ordinary people; you will be able to do it only in heaven. What you can and should do during the time you use for occupations other than prayer alone is to keep the thought of me as actively before your mind as you can and the nature of your work permits, lifting up the eyes of your soul towards me as often and as lovingly as possible. Then you will be praying to me as ceaselessly and continually as it is possible for poor mortals to do.

"As you will see, prayer is primarily thinking of me with love—the more anyone loves me, the more he prays. Prayer is the atten-

tion of the soul lovingly fixed on me. The more loving that attention is, the better is the prayer." [23]

> *"But thou, when thou shalt pray,*
> *enter into thy chamber and having*
> *shut the door, pray to thy*
> *Father in secret."*
>
> Matt. 6:6

Our Lord is here giving us instruction in private prayer: shut-
ting ourselves in our rooms, we should pray there in solitude
to our Father who sees what is done in secret. So then, in addition to our well-loved prayer before the Blessed Sacrament, and
our common prayer, when our Lord stands in the midst of those
met together to pray to him, we should love and practise daily
private and secret prayer, in which no one sees us but our heavenly
Father, prayer in which we are all alone with him, in which no
one but us knows we are praying to him. This is the prayer of
intimacy, a delightful secret in which we freely unfold our hearts,
far from all prying eyes, at the knees of our Father.[24]

> *"He fell upon his face,*
> *praying and saying . . ."*
>
> Matt. 26:39

Our Lord fell upon his face to pray. We should imitate him,
preferring to pray prostrate or kneeling, in the most penitential
attitudes, the most humble, the most prayerful. These are, in any
case, the attitudes most fitting to us, as they are also those that
show the most love. What attitude could be more loving than

[23] From "Eight Days in Ephrem" (cf. ES, pp. 160–2).
[24] From "Meditations on Gospel Texts on the Principal Virtues" (cf.
ES, pp. 6 ff.).

kneeling at the feet of one's beloved? We should adopt it at the feet of our Beloved. We should not be afraid to sit in his presence, as St. Mary Magdalene did, or even to stand, but we should prefer to kneel and whenever possible should pray either kneeling or prostrate, following both his example to us as recorded in this text and the dictates of the humility, repentance and love that together make up our prayers.

> *"My Father, if it be possible, let this chalice pass from me. Nevertheless, not as I will, but as thou wilt."*
>
> Matt. 26:39

Our Lord is teaching us to pray. First we should ask God for what we want, doing so with the simplicity of a child asking something of its father. Then we should add: "Nevertheless, not as I will, but as thou wilt."

This then is what we must do. There must be nothing indirect in our prayers. They must be completely simple. We should ask for what our hearts desire, without wasting time wondering if we should do better to ask for something different; we must pray straightforwardly, in all simplicity, asking for what we want and adding: "Nevertheless, not as I will, but as thou wilt." [25]

> *"He went up into a mountain alone to pray. And when it was evening, he was there alone."*
>
> Matt. 14:23

Our Lord prayed alone and during the night. It was his custom to do so. The Gospel tells us many times, "and at night he went alone to pray."

[25] *Ibid.* (cf. ES, pp. 18 ff.).

Following his example, we should love to pray at night and alone, cherishing such prayer and making a practice of it. We all find it pleasant to be alone with one we love in the midst of silence, when all the world is asleep and darkness covers the earth. How much more pleasant it is, then, to go and spend these hours alone with God. They are hours of incomparable happiness, the blessed hours that led St. Anthony to find the night all too short. Then are the hours when, while everything is silent and asleep, while everything is drowned in darkness, I live at the feet of my God, pouring out my heart in love of him, telling him I love him, while he tells me I shall never love him as much as he loves me, however great my love may be. Those nights are blessed which my God allows me to spend in intimate converse with him. O my Lord and my God, let me realize as fully as I should the value of such moments! Make me *delectare in Domino*.[26] Following your example, let me know no moments more precious, no rest more genuine, no sweeter and more jealously sought hours than those I spend in prayer at night and alone.[27]

> *"What? Could you not watch one hour with me?"*
> Matt. 26:40

O God, you were not speaking here only to your apostles, but to all those who, though able to watch with you, to give their company through the night to your anguished heart, to console you by loyally and lovingly watching and praying with you, yet do not do so, but give themselves up to sleep, being short of courage and thus of love. They do not realize the value of watching with you. They do not understand that watching at your feet is an incomparable joy, a happiness of which even the saints and angels

[26] "Delight in the Lord" (cf. Ps. 37:4).
[27] From "Meditations on Gospel Texts on the Principal Virtues" (cf. ES, pp. 8–9).

are not worthy. They do not rejoice to be in your presence, as one rejoices to be in the presence of someone one loves passionately, and they do not long passionately to console you and relieve your agony. If they were to long to console you with the passion they ought to show, they would never yield to a temptation as base and brutish as sleep. If they were as conscious as they should be of the infinite joy of praying at your feet, in your presence, would they not stay praying to you indefinitely, not noticing that time was passing, having only one fear in their joy—the fear of seeing it come to an end?

Alas, O God, how often I am one of these base, low, despicable beings who so often fall asleep at your feet and give themselves up to slumber when they could be praying with you. Forgive, oh forgive me! Help me, O God, so that I may never again fall into such hateful and cold indifference, into such unworthy disloyalty! I have so often fallen. I hate my sin. I regard it with horror. My God, I pray you with all my soul: Forgive me! [28]

HOLINESS   Luke 12:48

"And you, my darlings, my favorites, my privileged ones, my best beloved, remember, my chosen ones, those important words I said to you: 'Unto whomsoever much is given, of him much shall be required.' They were said for you, my chosen ones, on whom so much has been heaped—you to whom I said everything and gave everything, who have received so much and so many graces. The more you have received, the more will be asked of you. The magnitude of the favors I have done for you is a sign I myself have given you of the magnitude of the sanctity that will be asked of you. So then, do not be foolish enough to believe that it is proud to long for, hope for and wish to attain

[28] *Ibid.* (cf. ES, pp. 19 ff.).

a very high level of sanctity. So far is it from being pride that it is, on the contrary, a duty and an obligation. The graces I have heaped on you and which, unless you are ungrateful, you cannot fail to acknowledge, are of a kind specially selected by me to lift you up to greater sanctity. When I give great graces to a soul, it is as though I was saying, 'I want you to become very holy. I shall ask you to account for the great graces I have given you.'

"However little shadow of justification you have, the accumulation of my graces, and my favors cannot fail to make humility and fear grow in you. Far from puffing you up with pride, the more you receive, the more you will be filled with fear, and the more you will be humbled by thoughts of your profound lowliness. If you are in your right mind, what you ought to fear more than pride is discouragement. This discouragement would in fact appear if I had not made it your duty to hope always, and to believe in spite of everything in my infinite mercy, casting yourself blindly onto my Heart, however worthless you may think yourself, as the prodigal son threw himself on the heart of his father.[29]

Brother Charles longed to come to know Jesus as intimately as possible, and in order to do so he scrutinized his every step so as to be able to imitate him more perfectly. Taken together the following series of extracts from his meditations make up a kind of Life of Jesus.

THE VISITATION   Luke 1:39

[*Jesus speaks:*] "I had scarcely taken flesh when I asked my mother to take me to the house where John was to be born, so that I might sanctify him before his birth. In the Incarnation, I gave myself to the world for its salvation. Even before my birth

[29] From "Eight Days at Ephrem" (cf. ES, pp. 162 ff.).

I was working at my task, the sanctification of mankind—and I moved my mother to work at it with me. She is not the only one I have ever moved to work at the sanctification of souls from the first moment of being given to them: I do the same in every soul to which I give myself. On one occasion I said to my apostles, 'Preach,' and I gave them their mission and laid down rules for their fulfillment of it.

"Here and now I am saying to other souls—to all those who have been given me and now lead hidden lives, possessing me without having been given a mission to preach—I tell them to sanctify souls by silently carrying me among them. To souls in silence, leading the hidden life in solitude far from the world, I say, 'All, all, of you, work for the sanctification of the world; work in the world as my Mother did, wordlessly, silently; go and set up your devotional retreats in the midst of those who do not know me; carry me among them by setting up an altar among them, a tabernacle, carrying the Gospel to them not by word of mouth but by the persuasive force of example, not by speaking, but by living; sanctify the world, carry me into the world, all you pious souls living a hidden and silent life—as Mary carried me to John.' " [30]

THE NATIVITY AND CIRCUMCISION   Luke 2:7; 2:21

"I was born, born for you, in a cave, in December, in the cold, homeless, in the middle of a winter's night, in the unheard-of poverty of the extremely poor, in solitude, in an abandonment unique in this world. What, my children, do I want you to learn from my birth? *To believe in my love,* to believe that I have loved you until now. To hope in me, who have loved you so dearly. I want to teach you to *despise the world,* which was so unimportant to me. I want to teach you *poverty, lowliness, soli-*

[30] "Eight Days in Ephrem" (cf. ES, pp. 128 ff.).

tude, humility, penance. I want to teach you to love me, for I was not content with giving myself to the world in the Incarnation, sanctifying it invisibly in the Visitation; no, that did not satisfy my love. From the moment of my birth onwards, I showed myself to you, giving myself wholly to you, putting myself in your hands. From then on, you could touch me, hear me, possess me, serve me, console me. Love me now; I am so close to you.

"In my unimaginable goodness, I did not merely give myself to you at my birth for a few hours or years: I am still in your hands, and shall be henceforth until the end of the world. Think of the unending good fortune I brought you in my birth: the ability to *serve me*—to serve me by serving the Church, to serve me by serving your neighbor, to serve me myself, living there near you in the tabernacle. Not only can you serve me, you can also *console* me. I watched you at every moment of your life, at every moment of my own, and my human Heart, which loves you so fondly, has rejoiced or suffered at each of these moments, rejoicing if they were devoted to good, suffering if they were used to do evil.

"How happy you should be to be able to console me at every moment of your lives! By becoming so small, so gentle a child, I was crying out to you: *Have trust! Come close to me!* Do not be afraid of me, come to me, take me in your arms, adore me. But when you adore me, give me what children need: loving embraces. Do not be afraid, do not be so frightened in the presence of such a gentle baby, smiling at you and holding out his arms to you. He is your God, but he is all smiles and gentleness. Do not be afraid. Be all fondness, love and trust, and—let me add—obedience. Obedience not only directly to God, but also indirectly, by obeying for his sake, and as though they were himself, all those he has given you to be your preceptors: your parents, ecclesiastical superiors, spiritual directors, superiors of whatever kind, obeying them all in whatever degree God tells you to do. . . .

"In my circumcision, too, it was my desire to teach you obedience with humility—perfect obedience to all the commandments of the Church, whether great or small; unquestioning obedience, without discussion about the usefulness of the command, obedience for obedience's sake.

"I also wished to teach you *penance,* and at the same time give you a little love: the penance I did in embracing this suffering, the love I showed as early as the eighth day of my life in seizing this opportunity to pour out my blood for you.

"It was my desire to be called Jesus, primarily because the name is *true,* possessing that truth you ought so much to love— and also because it is profoundly tender and gentle and so wonderfully expressive of my *love* for you; finally because it is a name to inspire you to *trust* in me, to offer me your hand freely and easily, as to your Saviour, so that you will always turn to me with the utmost trust, with complete abandonment. And that is what I want to see in you. A hundred times over I have called myself your Father, and have been a father to you. I want you, when you adore me as God, to love me as a son and a brother, with devotion and trust." [31]

THE HIDDEN LIFE OF JESUS

> *"They returned into Galilee,*
> *to their city Nazareth."*
>
> Luke 2:39

"After my presentation and my flight into Egypt, I withdrew to Nazareth. There I spent the years of my childhood and youth, till I was thirty years of age. Once again, it was for your sake I went there, *for love of you.* What was the meaning of that part of my life? I led it for your instruction. I instructed you continually

[31] From "Eight Days in Ephrem" (cf. ES, pp. 131–4).

for thirty years, not in words, but by my silence and example. What was it I was teaching you? I was teaching you primarily that it is possible to do good to men—great good, infinite good, divine good—without using words, without preaching, without fuss, but by silence and by giving them a good example. What kind of example? The example of devotion, of duty towards God lovingly fulfilled, and goodness towards all men, loving kindness to those about one and domestic duties fulfilled in holiness. The example of poverty, lowliness, recollection, withdrawal: the obscurity of a life hidden in God, a life of prayer, penance and withdrawal, completely lost in God, buried deep in him. I was teaching you to live by the labor of your own hands, so as to be a burden on no one and to have something to give to the poor. And I was giving this way of life an incomparable beauty—the beauty of being a copy of mine.

"Everyone who wants to be perfect must live *in poverty,* imitating with the utmost fidelity my poverty at Nazareth. How clearly I preached *humility* at Nazareth, by spending thirty years in obscure labors, and *obscurity* by remaining so completely unknown for thirty years—I who am the light of the world—and *obedience,* in that I, who am God, made myself subject for thirty years to my parents who, although unquestionably holy, were human beings nonetheless. Having seen me be so obedient so long to those to whom I owed no obedience whatsoever, whose sovereign Master, Creator and Judge I was, how can you refuse perfect obedience to those of whom I, your God, have said: 'He that heareth you, heareth me'? [32]

"How little esteem I showed of the things of this world, of human greatness, and the ways of the world, of everything the world holds dear: nobility, wealth, status, knowledge, cleverness, repute, honor, worldly distinction, good manners. I pushed all

[32] Luke 10:16.

these things far away from me, so that I should be seen only as a poor laborer living very devoutly, completely withdrawn from the world." [33]

*

Luke 2:51

My Jesus, you are so close to me: inspire in me the thoughts I should have about your hidden life.

"And he went down with them and came to Nazareth and was subject to them." He went down, he humbled himself—his life was one of humility. Being God, you took the appearance of a man; as a man, you made yourself the least of men. Your life was one of *lowliness:* the place you took was the lowest of all. You went down *with them* to live their life with them, the life of the poor laborer, living by working. Your life, like theirs, was one of *work and poverty.* They were obscure, and you lived in the shadow of their *obscurity.* You went to *Nazareth,* a forgotten little town, hidden in the hills, from where, it was commonly said, nothing good ever came. This was real withdrawal, far from the world and its great cities. And you lived in this state of *retirement.*

You *were subject to them*—subject as a son is to his father and mother. Your life was one of *submission,* filial submission. You were obedient in every way that a good son is obedient. If your parents had wanted anything that was not in harmony with your divine vocation you would not have done it. You obeyed "God rather than men," as you did when you remained behind in Jerusalem for three days. But except when your vocation required you not to submit yourself to their wishes, you were obedient to them in all things; you were the best of sons in every way. Therefore

[33] From "Eight Days in Ephrem" (cf. ES, pp. 135 ff.).

you were not only obedient to their least wishes, but you forestalled them, doing whatever would please them, console them, make their life pleasant and acceptable to them, striving with all your heart to make them happy, being a model son, doing everything possible for them—insofar as your vocation allowed. But your vocation was to perfection, and you, O Son of God, could not be anything but perfect. . . .

This was your life at Nazareth—here, where I have the infinite good fortune, the unparalleled grace of living! For this I render all my thanks.

Your life was that of a model among sons—and you lived it with a mother and father who were both poor working people. This was one half of your life, the part turned towards the world while it filled heaven with a celestial perfume. It was the visible part of your life. The invisible part was your life in God, a life of unceasing contemplation. You worked, consoled your parents, conversing with them with the utmost fondness and holiness, praying with them throughout the day. But you prayed too in the solitude and darkness of the night; your soul was poured out in silence.

You were always, always, praying, at every moment—for to pray is to be with God, and you were God. But far into the nights your human soul prolonged that contemplation, and it was united closely at every moment of the day with your divinity. Your life was one continual outpouring into God, a continual gazing at God, unending contemplation of God at every moment of your life.

And what kind of prayer was it that made up the half of your life in Nazareth? First and above all it was *adoration*, that is, *contemplation*, that silent adoration which is the most eloquent of prayers: *Tibi silentium laus*.[34] It was that kind of silent adoration which confirms a declaration of love most passionately, just as love expressed in wondering admiration is the most ardent love.

---

[34] "Give praise in silence."

Then, secondly—in second place and occupying less time—it was *thanksgiving:* thanksgiving first for the divine glory, for the fact that God is God, then thanksgiving for the graces bestowed on the world and all created things. Then a cry for *forgiveness,* forgiveness for all the sins committed against God, forgiveness for those who do not ask for it themselves, an act of contrition for the whole world, an act of sorrow at seeing God offended. Then *petition,* asking for the glory of God, that God might be glorified by all created things, that his reign among them might begin, that his will might be done among them as it is among the angels, and that these lowly creatures might be given everything, whether spiritual or temporal, that they need, and might finally be freed from all evil both in this world and the next. And petition, too, asking that graces might be poured especially abundantly on those who, by the divine will, lived close to Jesus and around him: his mother and father, his cousins and friends, those who loved him and clung to him.[35]

TEMPTATION IN THE DESERT   Luke 4:12

"I allowed the devil to tempt me in the desert. I did it for your sakes, from love of you, for your instruction; first, so that you should know that temptation is stronger in the desert than elsewhere, and so that those who withdraw into solitude for love of me should be neither surprised nor discouraged by the numerous temptations they experience; and second, so that you should realize that temptation is not sin, for I myself was tempted—and tempted by monstrous ideas (therefore you should be neither saddened nor discouraged when you are tempted; neither should you despise your friends or blame them when they are). And lastly I was tempted so that you could see how to resist temptations. They must be resisted immediately, as soon as they make

[35] From Retreat at Nazareth (cf. ES, pp. 56–60).

themselves apparent, from the very first instant. An excellent way of combating them is to bring the words of Holy Scripture into play against them, for by nature of their origin the strength of these words is divine." [36]

THE PUBLIC MINISTRY

O my Lord Jesus, how pleasant it will be to spend the whole day again thinking about you! It should fill all my days. When I work, or pray, or talk, the whole time except when I am asleep, I am praying and should be thinking of you, looking at you just because you are there. I do it very badly, but I long so much to do it better that I hope to achieve it with your grace: Give me that grace! But today it is not enough merely to do that: I must not only look at you, I must do nothing except look at you. What happiness you have been good enough to give me and how happy I am!

My God, here am I at your feet in my cell. It is night, everything is quiet, everything is sleeping. At this moment I am perhaps the only one in Nazareth at your feet. What have I done to deserve such graces? How I thank you and how happy I am! I adore you from the depths of my heart, my God. I adore you with all my soul, and love you with all the strength that is in my heart. I am yours, yours alone; my whole being is yours. It is yours in any case, whatever I might think, and yours by choice, the free choice of my whole heart. Do with me as seems pleasing to you. Let me make this retreat in a way that is pleasing to you. "Be perfect, as your heavenly Father is perfect" is your reply to me. Very well, O God, make me carry it out as perfectly as possible, in you, through you and for you. Amen.

What was the manner of your public life, my Lord Jesus?

"I strove to save men through speech and works of mercy, in-

[36] From "Eight Days at Ephrem" (cf. ES, pp. 136 ff.).

stead of being satisfied to save them by prayer and penance alone as I had been doing at Nazareth. My zeal for souls became externally apparent.

"Yet while my life became very public, it still preserved some of the qualities of the solitary life (I often withdrew for a night, or for several whole days into solitude to pray). It remained a life of *prayer, penance* and *interior recollection.* And apart from the time devoted to preaching the Gospel, it was a life of *solitude.*

"It was a *tiring* life. Continual journeying, long discourses, withdrawals into the desert without shelter were not accomplished without weariness.

"It was a life of *physical suffering:* the inclemency of the weather, nights passed without shelter, meals taken irregularly, whenever work allowed—all these things led to suffering. Then there were *spiritual sufferings:* the ingratitude of human beings, their deafness to my voice, their ill will, their hardness of heart, all the spiritual and bodily miseries of men brought to my immediate notice every day. The smallness of the numbers of those being saved and the vast total of the damned; human sufferings, the sufferings of the just—those of my own Mother, the prospect of my own passion, continually growing nearer and clearer, the persecution and hatred aroused by my saving words and the love I offered all men, and above all the ingratitude of that "unfaithful and perverse generation"—all these things made my Heart groan with love and compassion.

"Then again, it was a life of *persecution:* I was persecuted by everyone everywhere, in Jerusalem as in Nazareth; they wanted to stone me and throw me down from a high place; everywhere, in towns and villages, Pharisees, Scribes, Sadducees, Herodians, all sought to destroy me, setting snares for me, insulting me both privately and publicly, calling me possessed, a devil, a traitor, an impostor, denouncing me to the priests. The Gentiles despised me just as the Israelites did. Everywhere my life was threatened, either by Herod or by the Pharisees. I was forced to fly from place to place. Several times they tried to seize me and it was only by a miracle that I saved myself.

"It was a time when I had to be courageous before men, reproving them openly for their sins, even chastising them, unmasking hypocrites publicly, preaching the doctrine of God in the presence of those who could argue fiercely and powerfully against it, proclaiming the truth before an angry crowd ready to reject it; doing the very works of which I was later to be accused and condemned in the very Temple and synagogues themselves. What courage it took to speak in the Temple at Jerusalem to people who always had stones to hand ready to stone me, and in the synagogue at Nazareth where the Pharisees ground their teeth in anger against me and made a thousand plots to destroy me!

"Love of the truth: I was never without it, I who am myself Truth. But I demonstrated it clearly in spreading it zealously abroad when surrounded by so many dangers and troubles—how clearly I demonstrated its worth!

"Humility: I was humble when I had myself baptized by John, when I forbade my disciples so often to proclaim that I was the Son of God, when I hid the blessings I gave, the miracles I performed, when so often I told those I healed to speak of it to no one. I showed humility when I, the Almighty, fled from town to town when I was persecuted, although I could have annihilated my enemies (and justly, too) with a word." [37]

●

Time is passing, O God, and the hours are flowing away. Another day is ended, another night begun. Only a few days are left to you here below; few nights to lie at your feet. Where will you be twenty-five days from now? Alas, my God, you will no

[37] Retreat at Nazareth (cf. ES, pp. 60–3).

longer be alive, and in what pain you will have said farewell to life! It was for our sakes alone that you came down, O God. And human beings, having rejected you from your birth are going to thrust you out of this world in the midst of the most dreadful torments. That is how this world receives its God and men their Saviour and Creator!

It is true that to enter into your glory you must leave the world. And it is right that you should stop being the man of sorrows to become the king of glory. But, O God, what a flood of torments you will pass through before taking your place at the right hand of your Father! Men did not accept you when you came into the world: every door in Bethlehem was closed to you at your birth. You were scarcely more than a few days old before they began to hunt you to kill you. During the next thirty years, you were left in peace only because you remained hidden first in a foreign country, then in a little town lost in the mountains, buried in silence and lowliness. As soon as you broke your silence, they began to persecute you: first, your fellow townsmen wanted to put you to death, then after you had been preaching for three years, being threatened with death continually from all sides, you allowed your murder to be done. That is how the world received its God!

Yet you, O God, did not curse it, but left it with a blessing. You still bless it every day, and will go on blessing it millions of times a day until the end of the ages. And you heap signal graces upon it, and will continue to heap them up. And you will return to it—and more, not only will you return to it in the future, you are in it now until the end of the ages, present not only in one place, but in a multitude of places. But now the hour of your going is about to strike. I thank you, my God, for having been allowed to lie at your feet.[38]

[38] From "Eight Days in Ephrem" (cf. ES, pp. 129–31).

> *"Sit you here till I*
> *go yonder and pray."*
> Matt. 26:36

What did our Lord do during the last hours before his arrest
and the beginning of his passion? He went apart alone to pray.
So we, too, when we have a grave trial to undergo, or danger or
suffering to face, should spend the last moments, the last hour
separating us from it in prayer, solitary prayer. When we are faced
with any serious happening in our lives, this is what we should
do, preparing ourselves for it, seeking strength, enlightenment and
grace to behave well in it by using the last hour, the last moment
between us and it in prayer, in praying alone.[39]

THE SUFFERINGS OF JESUS

You want me to meditate on your passion, my God. Inspire my
thoughts yourself, for such images always leave me powerless.

The passion—what memories! The knocks and blows from the
high priests' servants: "Prophesy . . . who is he that struck
thee?" Silence before Herod and Pilate; the scourging; crowning
with thorns; the way of the cross; the crucifying; the cross. "Father,
into thy hands I commend my spirit." What visions, O God, what
images! And if I love you, then *what tears!* What *remorse* when I
remember it was to make fitting expiation for my sins that you
suffered so. How deeply I am moved when I remember that you
faced these torments, even willed them, to prove your love for me,
to proclaim it down the centuries. O the remorse I feel for having
loved you so little! The remorse of having done so little penance

[39] "Meditations on Gospel Texts on the Principal Virtues" (cf. ES, p.
17). Charles de Foucauld spent the last hours before his violent death
in the silence he recommends here.

for the sins for which you performed such a penance as this. How greatly I long to love you at last, in my turn, and prove my love to you in every possible way.

What ways are there, O God, how I can love you? How can I tell you I love you? "He who loves me is he who keeps my commandments . . . Greater love than this no man hath, that a man lay down his life for his friends." To fulfill your commandments (*mandata*) is to fulfill not only your orders but also your counsels, to follow your least piece of advice, follow your example in the smallest things. One of your most important counsels was that we should imitate you: "Follow me . . . they that follow me walk no longer in darkness . . . I have given you an example that as I have done to you, so you do also . . . It is enough for the disciple that he be as his master." While we live, we must follow as accurately as possible all the instructions and examples you gave; then we must die for your Name: that is how we can love you and prove to you that we love you—it is the way you yourself described for us in the Gospel, O God.

Love, O God, asks yet one more thing, and the Gospel also tells me of it, not by words, but by the example of the Blessed Virgin and St. Mary Magdalene at the foot of the cross: *Stabat Mater*.[40] Compassion, weeping for your sufferings, is indeed also a grace: faced with the spectacle of your cross, I cannot by my own power draw cries of grief from my stony heart, for, alas, it has become terribly hard! But at least I can ask you for compassion: I owe it to you, but if I am to be able to give it to you, I must first ask you for it. I have to ask you for everything I owe you.

My God, from the depths of your mercy, from the treasury of your mystical and infinite goodness, you have given me the great

[40] Beginning of the Sequence on the feast of the Seven Sorrows of the Blessed Virgin, September 15. Cf. John 19:25.

grace of living under that sky and in that land where you lived, of walking over the very ground you walked over—and, alas, watered with your tears, sweat and blood. Do not leave me tearless as I visit the places that witnessed your sufferings; do not leave me tearless when I kiss the path your footsteps trod in Gethsemane, along the Way of Sorrows, to the pretorium and Cavalry. Give me a heart of flesh in place of my heart of stone, and because you have given me this inexpressible grace, let me kiss this most holy soil, let me kiss it with my heart and my soul, and with the tears you want me to have, the tears I ought to have, O my Lord, my King, my Master, my Beloved, my Saviour, my God!

I resolve: To ask for martyrdom, long for it, and if it pleases God, suffer it in order to love Jesus with a greater love;

To have zeal for souls, a burning love for the salvation of souls —which have all been ransomed at so unique a price;

To despise no one, but to desire the greatest good for everyone, because everyone is covered by the blood of Jesus as though by a cloak;

To do what I can for the salvation of souls, in whatever way my situation allows, because they all cost Jesus so much and were all—and still are—so greatly loved by him;

To be perfect, to be holy myself, for Jesus held me so dear that he gave his love for me;

To have a great longing for perfection, to believe that when my confessor orders me to do some particular thing, I can do anything, for everything is possible to God's glory. How could God refuse me just one grace when he has already given all his blood for me?

To have an infinite horror of sin and the imperfection that leads to it, because it has already cost Jesus so dear;

To suffer when I see others sin and God offended, because sin is so horrible to him that he chose to expiate it by such torments;

To have absolute trust in the love of God, an inextinguishable faith in his love, because he has proved it to me by being willing to suffer such pains for me;

To be humble at the thought of all he has done for me, and the little I have done for him;

To long for sufferings to give him love for love, and imitate him, and not be crowned with roses whereas he was crowned with thorns, to expiate the sins of mine he has already expiated with such suffering, to share in his work, offering myself with him in sacrifice—though I am nothing—as a victim for the sanctification of men.[41]

> *"Stay you here and watch with me."*
> Matt. 26:38

Was our Lord saying these words only to his apostles? No, he was speaking to us all, all those he loves, all those he was thinking about during his agony—all of us whose loyal and loving company is consolation to him in these painful moments. Let us then be loyal to the practice of "watching" with him every Thursday evening, keeping him company, supporting him, consoling him, being with him wholeheartedly in his agony. The Thursday evening vigil with our Lord in agony should be one of the practices to which we are faithful throughout our lives. For love of our Lord's Heart we should never fail to be there. He is asking it of us formally in these words addressed to his apostles. Can we fail him? [42]

> *"And being in an agony,*
> *he prayed the longer."*
> Luke 22:43

[41] Retreat at Nazareth (cf. ES, pp. 63–7).
[42] From "Meditations on Gospel Texts on the Principal Virtues" (cf. ES, p. 17 ff.).

O God, I beseech you, let us follow your example. The more we suffer and the more we are tempted, the more we should pray. In prayer is our only help, our only strength, our only consolation. We pray that the pain and power of temptation will not paralyze our prayer. The devil puts forth all his strength to stop it at such times. But far from yielding to this temptation, far from yielding to the natural weakness that would like to see the soul absorbed in its pain and conscious of nothing else, we must look for our Saviour who is there, close to us, and we must talk with him. He is before us, looking lovingly upon us, straining to hear us, telling us to speak to him, telling us that he is there, that he loves us. And we have no word for him, not a glance to give him. How unworthy! Let us gaze on him, talk to him constantly, as one does when one is in love, as our Lord is doing now to his Father. The deeper into agony we fall, the more necessary it is for us to throw ourselves into the embrace of our Beloved, pressing ourselves against him in uninterrupted prayer. O God, give me this grace—the grace to follow your example by fulfilling so compelling and sweet a duty.

> *"Father, into thy hands*
> *I commend my spirit."*
> Luke 23:46

This was the last prayer of our Master, our Beloved. May it also be ours. And may it be not only that of our last moment, but also of our every moment. "Father, I put myself in your hands; Father, I abandon myself to you, I entrust myself to you. Father, do with me as it pleases you. Whatever you do with me, I will thank you for it. Giving thanks for anything, I am ready for anything, I accept anything, give thanks for anything. As long as your will, my God, is done in me, as long as your will is done in all your creatures, in all your children, in all those your heart loves,

I ask for nothing else, O God. I put my soul into your hands. I give it to you, O God, with all the love of my heart, because I love you, and because my love requires me to give myself. I put myself unreservedly in your hands. I put myself in your hands with infinite confidence, because you are my Father." [43]

"It is consummated."
John 19:30

These are our Lord's last words to his Father cited in St. John. "I have done all you gave me to do." My God, may these words also be ours at our last hour—though they will not then have the same meaning and the same perfection. We are only worthless human beings; but granted our wretchedness, may they at least be ours as far as they can be.

What must I do if they are to be, O God? I must ask you what it is you have given me to do, and I must ask you—from whom alone strength comes—to do it. I beseech you, my Lord and my God, to let me see clearly what your will for me is. Then give me the strength to do it, fulfilling it loyally till the end, in thanksgiving and love.[44]

The Resurrection and Ascension

You are rising from the dead and going up into heaven. You are there, in your glory. You are suffering no longer, you will never suffer again. You are in bliss, and will be eternally. O God, loving you, how happy I ought to be! If what I care about above all things is your good, how I ought to rejoice, how pleased and

[43] *Ibid.* (cf. ES, p. 28 ff.).
[44] *Ibid.* (cf. ES, p. 35).

delighted I ought to be! You, my God, are in bliss for all eternity: you lack nothing; you are infinitely and eternally happy.

But I too am happy, my God, for I love you above all things. Because you are in bliss, I too can say I lack nothing, I am in heaven, I am blessed whatever happens, whatever may befall me.

A resolve: When we are unhappy, in despair over ourselves, or other people, or things, we must remember that Jesus is in glory, sitting at the right hand of the Father, blessed forever. And we must remember, too, that if we love him as we ought, the beatitude of the infinite being will be acting continually in our souls on the unhappiness there—unhappiness originating in a finite being. Therefore our souls ought to be full of joy at the beatitude of our God, and the troubles that oppress them should vanish like clouds before the sun: for our God is in bliss. We should rejoice unceasingly, for the evils suffered by creatures are minute beside the Creator's bliss.

There will always be unhappiness in our lives, and it is right that there should be: unhappiness for the sake of the love we bear —and rightly bear—ourselves and all men, and for the sake, too, of the love we bear Jesus, and in memory of his sufferings. Then there will be the unhappiness caused by the longing we cannot but have for justice—that is, for the glory of God—and the pain we are bound to undergo when we see injustice, and God being insulted.

But right as these sufferings are, they should not last long in our souls. They should be transitory. What should endure and be *our normal state—the state to which we should constantly return— is joy in the glory of God,* joy at seeing that Jesus is suffering no longer, and will suffer no more, but is in bliss forever at the right hand of God.[45]

---

[45] Retreat at Nazareth (cf. ES, pp. 67 ff.).

JESUS IN THE HOLY EUCHARIST

Lord Jesus, you are in the Holy Eucharist. You are there, a yard away in the tabernacle. Your body, your soul, your human nature, your divinity, your whole being is there, in its twofold nature. How close you are, my God, my Saviour, my Jesus, my Brother, my Spouse, my Beloved!

You were not nearer to the Blessed Virgin during the nine months she carried you in her womb than you are to me when you rest on my tongue at Holy Communion. You were no closer to the Blessed Virgin and St. Joseph in the caves at Bethlehem or the house at Nazareth or during the flight into Egypt, or at any moment of that divine family life than you are to me at this moment— and so many others—in the tabernacle. St. Mary Magdalene was no closer to you when she sat at your feet at Bethany than I am here at the foot of this altar. You were no nearer to your apostles when you were sitting in the midst of them than you are to me now, my God. How blessed I am!

It is wonderful, my Lord, to be alone in my cell and converse there with you in the silence of the night—and you are there as God, and by your grace. But to stay in my cell when I could be before the Blessed Sacrament—why, it would be as though St. Mary Magdalene had left you on your own when you were at Bethany to go and think about you alone in her room! It is a precious and devout thing, O God, to go and kiss the places you made holy during your life on earth—the stones of Gethsemane and Calvary, the ground along the Way of Sorrows, the waves of the sea of Galilee—but to prefer it to your tabernacle would be to desert the Jesus living beside me, to leave him alone, going away alone to venerate the dead stones in places where he is no longer. It would be to leave the room he is in—and with it his divine companionship—to go to kiss the floor of a room he was in, but is in no longer. To leave the tabernacle to go and venerate statues would be to leave the Jesus living at my side to go into another room to greet his portrait.

Is it not true that someone in love feels that he has made perfect use of all the time he spends in the presence of his beloved? Apart from then, is not that time used best which is employed in doing the will or furthering the welfare of his beloved in some other place?

"Wherever the sacred Host is to be found, there is the living God, there is your Saviour, as really as when he was living and talking in Galilee and Judea, as really as he now is in heaven. Never deliberately miss Holy Communion. Communion is more than life, more than all the good things of this world, more than the whole universe: it is God himself, it is I, Jesus. Could you prefer anything to me? Could you, if you love me at all, however little, voluntarily lose the grace I give you in this way? Love me in all the breadth and simplicity of your heart." [46]

JESUS LIVING IN THE CHURCH
AND IN THE FAITHFUL SOUL

My Lord Jesus, you are with us "to the consummation of the world," not only in the Holy Eucharist, but also through your grace. Your grace is in the Church, it dwells and lives in every loyal soul. The Church is your bride; the soul of every faithful Christian is also your bride. What effect does your grace have in them? It shapes them according to your pattern. Your grace is working unceasingly in the Church, making it more perfect: more perfect in the growing number of the saints, new saints

[46] *Ibid.* (cf. ES, pp. 69 ff.).

being continually added to the old, so that every day the crown of saints is made more nearly complete by the addition of new diamonds; more perfect, also, by the ever clearer exposition of its dogmas, and the ever more perfect arrangement of its liturgy and discipline.

It is made more perfect, too, by the new crosses you lay on it every day and the victories it wins daily against the Prince of this world; more perfect again by the persecutions it undergoes century after century—by which, through the sufferings it endures, it is made ever more like its Spouse. It is made more perfect still by the mass of merits added daily by its members to the merits of the day before. It is a great body of holiness, growing unceasingly, new glory to God added daily to the old, still living in the presence of God. It is made more perfect by the multitude of Holy Sacrifices, tabernacles, Communions in which this world daily offers Jesus to God, new offerings being added to the old; more perfect again because today's grace is added to yesterday's and cannot fail to bring the Bride closer step by step to her Spouse.

Jesus is the Church's soul. He gives everything the soul gives the body; he gives it *life,* immortal life, by making it immovable, and *light,* by making it infallible when it makes a statement about truth. *He works through it* and by means of it continues the work he began in the flesh while he lived among men: the glorification of God by the sanctification of men. This work is the purpose of the Church, as it was Christ's, and Jesus accomplishes it in the Church unceasingly through all the centuries.

You dwell in the faithful soul, my Lord: "We shall come to it, and make our dwelling with it." You become, as it were, the soul's soul; your grace supports it in all situations, enlightens its understanding, guides its will. It is no longer the soul that does things, but you in it. You give it life, the life of grace, the seed of the life in glory, in growing abundance. You give it truth, firmly establishing it in it, giving it a taste for it, opening its eyes to it, making it see things with the eyes of faith. And in this way you give it divine light, far above the darkness of this world. You continue your work in it. The purpose of every man—like that of the Church, and your own, my Lord Jesus—is to give glory to God (that is, to manifest his glory outwardly) and bring sanctification to men.

You love us. The more perfect we become, the greater will be your consolation. We should long to give you all possible consolation, for your commandment is that we should love you with all our strength. We should want to be as perfect as possible—so make our thoughts, words and actions like your own. Live in us, rule in us, so that it may be no longer we who live, but you in us, my God. Use our bodies and souls, which we give you unreservedly, continuing through them your life and work in this world, the glorification of God and the sanctification of men, as you yourself laid down in your eternal design, in you, through you and for you. Amen. Amen. Amen.[47]

Brother Charles would often turn his gaze on Jesus as Saviour, the Good Shepherd, going in search of strayed sheep, who bids us follow his example, becoming saviours with him.

THE GOOD SHEPHERD   Luke 15:4

"I am the Good Shepherd, constantly in search of strayed sheep. *Love me*—I have said those words to you a hundred times, because I love you so much, O my sheep, all of you. And *love one another,* because your Shepherd loved you so tenderly. Be grateful for my painstaking search for you, my goodness in forgiving you, and my joy when I find you again.

"Help me in my work: follow me. Like me, working with me,

[47] Retreat at Nazareth (cf. ES, pp. 71–3).

each of you following the guidance of his spiritual director, make every effort to lead back as many strayed sheep as possible. Share my feelings, my suffering at seeing my sheep get lost, my joy when I find them again. Share my constancy, my hope, my indulgent search, never-ending belief in the possibility of their return, my indulgence in forgiving them. Share my tenderness towards them when they do return—far from reproaching and punishing them, I shower caresses upon them, taking them to my heart, as the father took the prodigal son.

"So then, hope always for the return of every soul living in the world to what is good; work for it always insofar as obedience allows, and be tender towards sinners who do return as you have seen me be to so many souls. Putting everything in a word: *Do for sinners what you would want me to do for you.*" [48]

> *"It is not the will of your Father who is in heaven that one of these little ones should perish."*
> Matt. 18:14

Our Lord came to seek what was lost. He left a number sheep already in the fold to hurry after one that had strayed. We should do as he did. And as our prayers are a force certain to gain what they request, we should use them to go out in search of sinners, using them to do the work for which our Divine Spouse came into this world.

If our vocation is not to the apostolic life, we ought to pray the more powerfully for their conversion. For then prayer is almost the only possible practical means we have of doing good to them, and of helping our Spouse in his work of saving his children and rescuing from mortal danger those he so passionately

[48] From "Eight Days at Ephrem" (cf. ES, pp. 167 ff.).

loves, whom in his treatment he bade us love as much as he does himself. And if our lives are devoted to the apostolate, our apostolate will be fruitful only if we pray for those we want to convert, for our Lord gives only to him who asks, opens only to him who knocks. If God is to put effective words on our lips, inspire our hearts with good ideas, and to put good-will into the souls of those we approach, we need the grace of God. And we must ask for it if we are to receive it. So then, whatever our way of life may be, let us pray a great deal for the conversion of sinners, for it was for them above all that our Lord worked, suffered and prayed.

Let us pray every day with all our hearts for the salvation and sanctification of the lost but beloved children of our Lord, so that they may not perish, but may be blessed. Let us spend a long time every day in prayer for them with our whole hearts, so that our Lord's heart may be consoled by their conversion and rejoice in their salvation.[49]

Brother Charles continued to live his humble, patient, hidden life at Nazareth. He lived in a small boarded hut where gardening tools were kept. He spent whole days and nights before the Blessed Sacrament. He ran errands for the convent. There was only one desire in his heart: to imitate Jesus of Nazareth.

On January 16, 1898 he wrote to the Abbé Huvelin, describing his life and revealing his heart's desires.

Monsieur l'Abbé, my beloved Father:

It is eight years ago today since I arrived at our Lady of the Snows, eight years ago yesterday since I embraced you for the last time, eight years ago tomorrow since I entered the community. They are important memories. There have been so many journeys

[49] From "Meditations on Gospel Texts on the Principal Virtues" (cf. ES, pp. 12 ff.).

and changes since then! Where is the *requies in saeculum saeculi?* [50] In Jesus and Jesus alone. That has been the message of all my stopping-places, and every step of my journeys.

In Jesus, through obedience—for the more ardent my longing to do his will, the more I feel that the only security for me, uncertain and fearful as I am, is in obedience. So I bless Jesus in his manger, at the foot of which I stay as long as I can at this holy season, from where he has put me into your hands, my dear father, and I beseech you to guide me ever more clearly in all things, so that I do whatever is pleasing to God, and am prevented from doing anything displeasing to him. Everything you tell me to do, I will do—everything.

My life flows on in a profound calm. During the day I work while it is light; in the morning and the evening and for part of the night, I read and pray. I chiefly read dogmatic theology and enjoy it greatly. In addition I read St. Teresa and the lives of the saints. I say my office so as to join in the prayer of the Church. Because it is in the fullest sense the *prayer of the Church*. That was why I took it up again. Saying it, and savoring those beautiful Psalms, is a consolation to me. I also say the rosary, and the Way of the Cross (I often do it very quickly—am I wrong to do it so quickly? How long ought I to devote to it?), and practise mental prayer.

Being without a clock, I do not know how long I sleep, but I sleep well, and in the evening I ask my guardian angel to wake me when it will be pleasing to God. I get up at first light. I think I sleep about five hours and a half on the average. On rising, I say matins, then I meditate by writing about the Holy Gospels and the Psalms until the Angelus. Then I go to church. I receive Holy Communion every day; I make my confession every week. I have a good confessor, a Franciscan whom I do not see except at my

[50] Words from the ceremony of reception into a religious community: "This is my rest forever" (Ps. 131:14).

confession. I know that you are guiding me and I am completely in your hands.

Sundays and holidays I spend all my time with infinite bliss in church, reading and meditating at the foot of the tabernacle in the quiet little chapel of the Poor Clares. I also read treatises on theology there—at the feet of Him they are talking about. I gaze at the tabernacle, and they are delightful days. Non-working days are frequent in this diocese, and the good Abbess has increased their number for me.

On feast days and Sundays I have the same meals as the nuns: coffee in the morning, dinner at midday and a collation in the evening—on other days I live on bread. Up till now I have been having two meals, but there is so little mortification in my life, I suffer so little, that since yesterday I have undertaken to have only one—as I did for so long in the Trappist Order—though only during the winter. From Easter till September 14,[51] I shall have two, as the Trappists do. Eating only bread, it does not matter what time I eat. I believe I am doing right in doing this little thing for God. I do not wear a hair shirt and do not want to do so, but if you advise me to wear one, I will. My only mortification is the discipline. . . .

Fundamentally, my confessions always consist of: *lukewarmness* (prayer said badly, Office said badly, Mass heard very badly, little care taken to preserve the presence of God during the day, and so on); *sloth* (laziness over rising—I go back to sleep again sometimes, instead of rising the first time I wake); *gluttony* (I eat too much); *lack of charity* (not praying enough and fervently enough for my neighbor, not being firmly enough accustomed to seeing our Lord, seeing God's child, in everyone; uncharitable thoughts, passing strongly adverse judgments on people I knew

[51] The Feast of the Exaltation of the Holy Cross, the beginning of the monastic season of fast.

in other days when I do think of them); *pride* (not thinking of myself humbly enough, being over self-confident, allowing inflated thoughts and wishes about myself to arise); *not being repentant* enough for my past and present sins; *not being grateful* enough either to God or men. These are the most important things, especially *lukewarmness* and *sloth*.

I should tell you, however, that recently—and especially perhaps on the occasions of the anniversaries of my entering the Trappist Order and of my profession (February 2)—I have been tormented rather freqently by a thought with a foundation of *pride*: I sometimes tell myself that I would have been able to do good for souls by staying in the Trappist Order, that within two years I should have been the Superior; that with the help of the grace of God, I should have been able to do good in that little Trappist house at Akbès, whose position made it so suitable for the sanctification of its own monks and the people round about. I know very well that this is a temptation, there is nothing of what makes a superior in me: neither authority, nor stability, nor yet sound judgement or experience, knowledge or perspicacity—nothing at all. And the spirit of the Trappist Order—the *present* spirit is quite alien to me. . . . In my board hut at the foot of the Clarist's tabernacle, in my days of work and nights of prayer, I have had so completely what I have been looking and longing for over a period of eight years [52] that it is clear that God had prepared this place for me in his Nazareth. It had long been in my mind's eye; it is a good thing to be able to imitate in this way the hidden life of our Lord, sharing his obscurity and poverty.

But I still have this temptation. I can see it only as a trick of

[52] That is, since the beginning of his pilgrimage in the Holy Land (December 1888—January 1889). "I had envisaged, imagined, this life, walking through the streets of Nazareth, treading in the footsteps of our Lord, a poor workingman lost in lowliness and obscurity," he wrote in a letter to Madame de Bondy dated June 24, 1896 (quoted in TPF, p. 93).

the devil to torment me—or at least distract me for a lengthy period. But I am telling you about it so that you can see how much I need your encouragement and support, and so that you can see how much of a child I still am, constantly needing, really needing, your hand to hold on to, and even to be carried in your arms. My answer to the devil is that the life I am leading was good enough for our Lord for thirty years, so should it not satisfy me? If it satisfied the Blessed Virgin and St. Joseph all their lives, ought it not to satisfy me?

I have asked myself more than once if my theological reading might not have done something towards inducing these temptations to grandeur in me. But I am obliged to say that this reading has done me good, making me love the Church and my neighbor and correcting my views on a lot of points. Over the last four years it has truly transformed my interior life. It has taken nothing from me, but has rather given me a great deal. Philosophy has also been a great revelation to me. It, too, has done me a great deal of good. If you wish, I will read some more philosophy. If I hear nothing from you to the contrary, I shall continue with both sorts of reading. But if you see in it a shadow of danger for me, the slightest peril, tell me and I will stop it altogether. As I have already told you, noticing temptations to ambition appearing in myself, I have begun to fear that such reading might feed them and I have sometimes told myself it might be better to put aside reading of all kinds, together with ink and paper and even my breviary, and content myself with the rosary alone. But in this and every other matter, I shall do as you tell me. I have given you a picture of my life—now tell me what I should do. I shall obey you in everything.

Tell me, too, if there is anything I can do for the Poor Clares of Jerusalem. I pray God to accomplish his will in them, whatever it may be. If there is anything else I can do, tell me. Whatever happens to them will be in accordance with the will of God, but it is my duty to show my devotion to them. Pray for them. I often commend you to their prayers.

I hear that you are, alas, still in pain. May God glorify himself in you according to his will. If he would bring you some relief in your life here below, I should rejoice indeed. But God loves you and knows what is best for you. My beloved father, I pray for you more and more. I am with you more and more, and I pray for you constantly, especially as I know you are suffering. Bless your child kneeling with respect and such fond gratitude at your feet and loving you as your son in the Sacred Heart of our Lord Jesus Christ.

Brother Charles [53]

A few weeks later, on February 1, he wrote to the Abbé again:

The state of my soul is unchanged: I am always full of joy, rejoicing at the feet of Jesus. The simplicity of my life is profoundly pleasant to me, these long lonely hours of prayer and reading, spent so simply. I am quite overcome, and I marvel at the way God guides my soul. I realize how good for me my stay here is, and how *necessary it is to me*. I am dissolving and drowning in the peace of it, and I am profoundly astonished to see that, far from distracting me from union with Jesus, my reading and theology bring me to deeper participation in it. My interior life is one of union with Jesus at the different stages of his life in this world. Until tomorrow I shall be at Bethlehem; tomorrow morning [54] I am going to the Temple; tomorrow evening I shall leave during the night for Egypt. I shall be traveling with the Holy Family until Ash Wednesday, then I shall go with our Lord into

[53] Cf. ES, pp. 58–63.
[54] February 2, Candlemas Day; cf. the date of this letter.

the desert. A month before the end of Lent, I shall go to the raising of Lazarus at Bethany and be with our Lord during the last
part of his life, and then with his apostles from the Ascension till
Pentecost. From Pentecost till Advent, I work and pray with the
Holy Family at Nazareth.

That is my year—and as much as possible I stay at the feet
of the Blessed Sacrament: Jesus is there; it is as though I were
with his holy parents, or St. Mary Magdalene, sitting at his feet
at Bethany.

I am trying to profit from these graces and blessings, from this
peace, from the good air I am breathing, this beneficial solitude,
the healthy atmosphere in which I seem to be, by using it to
meditate and read and let God shape me.

As I have told you, I sometimes think I shall return to the
Trappists—something is driving me to it. I do not know whether
it is grace or temptation. You must judge. I can do no more
than tell you, so that, like a doctor, you can know what is to be
done and can smash my idea against a stone if you think it is a
bad one. You can offer me to God as he offered himself under
the form of a lamb "as it were, slain," [55] with no more self-will
than a dead body, like the tiny doves, "the offering of the poor," [56]
which were sacrificed on the day of the purification and were offered "in sacrifice" as I am in your hands.

The reasons why I am less settled in my present position than
I was at the beginning are, as far as I can see:

1. From the very fact that I made this sacrifice to God and
received from him this grace of *lowliness, poverty* and a livelihood gained humbly by *manual labor,* all this has come to seem
less valuable to me: "when someone has given away all the trea-
sures of his house, they are scorned as though he had given noth-

---

[55] Rev. 5:6.
[56] Cf. Luke 2:24 (Lev. 12:8).

ing." I wish to take back nothing and surrender nothing of all this, but while trying to keep it all, I should like to advance further. When I say "I should like" I mean that is what seems to be suggested by the vague aspirations I am trying to describe to you.

2. The more conscious I become of the value, the preciousness of poverty and lowliness, the more apparent it becomes to me that it would be better to *work*, enter the combat if need be, so that others may enjoy it, rather than enjoying it all alone.

3. Lastly, these very joys themselves, inasmuch as they are the joys peculiar to the position in which I find myself, make me want on the one hand *to work as hard as possible in the service of God,* while on the other they plunge me into *absolute indifference*, so that I have only one desire, that of doing his will, whatever it may be—and in absolute obedience to whatever you tell me. But when I consider how I can best serve God, it seems to me that: 1. I cannot do it more effectively than by re-entering a Trappist house and trying to arouse love there for the poverty, lowliness, public and mental prayer, and sacred studies in which God has been pleased to let me find the flowers of paradise; 2. God intends me for a Trappist house in the East; and 3. I must stay here for some time yet, in dear and blessed Nazareth—blessed a thousand times to me—a place I shall not leave without a great many tears, a true corner of heaven to me. If you could only imagine how good it is here, how pleasantly the days flow by with Jesus, Mary and Joseph. How happy I am here! It seems to me I ought to stay quite a long time in a place where my soul is in so good a state, where God shapes it, where it is given the strength it absolutely must have. It was sick indeed when I arrived; I have told you about it. In *everything, absolutely everything*, I will do what you tell me. I shall drive out the thoughts you tell me to drive out, and have those you tell me to have. I want to be "sacrificed" in your hands, like the young doves the Blessed Virgin will offer tomorrow. So

offer me "as it were, slain" to our beloved Jesus Christ, and bless this child, who is so truly yours and so joyful in having you for a father, and prays and prays for you and your poor health.

Your child who loves you in Jesus,

Brother Charles [57]

Although Brother Charles had left the Trappist Order, his relations with it were still good and he still had good friends in it.

On the Monday after the Feast of the Ascension, 1898, he wrote to Father Jerome, whom he had met at the Trappist house at Staouëli (in Algeria) and who was then studying at Rome:

Your task now is to live only with God alone, living until your priestly ordination as though you were alone with God in the universe. We must go through the desert and dwell there to receive the grace of God. It is while there that one expels from oneself everything that is not divine. The soul needs this silence, this recollection, this time to forget the created universe. It is during it that God establishes his kingdom in the soul and shapes its inner spirit, the spirit of intimate life with God, the soul's converse with God in faith, hope and charity. Later the soul will bring forth fruits strictly commensurate with the degree to which the inner man has been shaped within it. If there is no interior life, there will be no fruits—zeal, good intentions and hard work notwithstanding. It is a spring which would give sanctity to others, but cannot if it has none itself. One can not give what one does not have. It is in solitude, in life alone with God, in the recollection which is forgetful of everything created, that God gives himself wholly to him who thus gives himself wholly to God.[58]

[57] Cf. C, pp. 65–8.
[58] Cf. ES, p. 182.

On June 21, 1898, he wrote to this same priest again:

I hope that your life is continuing to be ever more lost, buried, engulfed in Jesus, with Mary and Joseph. You are now at that stage of life which symbolizes the infancy of Jesus. He learned to read at the knees of his holy parents. At that time he did not concern himself with the salvation of souls except in the interior pulses of his heart, where he was praying to God for the salvation of all mankind; but he was a little child and was not concerned about any one particular soul. He did not yet help Joseph with his work: he was too small. He learned to read at Mary's knee, sitting smiling at her feet, kissing her, gazing at her, keeping still and quiet. For several years, this life was enough for him—for the Son of God. May it be enough for you, my dear father, for it will be yours for several years: you are only five years old, you are learning to read, you have just begun to study, and obediently you are doing whatever you are told—as Jesus at five did everything his parents told him.

Later he will lead you out into the desert, and from there to Gethsemane—and to Calvary. But now you are living with Jesus, Mary and Joseph, as though you were alone with them in the world, by their poor hearth at Nazareth.[59]

In October 1898, Brother Charles was in Jerusalem, performing for the Poor Clares of the Holy City the same tasks as he had at Nazareth. The following are two letters he wrote on the 15th and 22nd of that month to the Abbé Huvelin:

Jerusalem, October 15, 1898

My beloved father:

I love writing to you on this, the Feast of St. Teresa when, during the last autumn I spent in the world, I heard you talking about

[59] Cf. ES, p. 183.

her to her daughters at Saint-Denis. May she bless you, dear father, obtaining for you what I also ask from her for myself, *the one thing necessary*: that we may glorify Jesus by loving him as much as possible.

How well I am placed here to think about that one thing necessary, for from my little window I can see Bethany, where these words fell from Jesus' lips.[60] You will remember perhaps that if you had not told me that God's will was that I should leave what little I had to my sister, I should have wanted to give it for a pious foundation at Bethany. It has pleased God to put that dear place under my windows, at about a mile's distance—and still without a single Catholic shrine. How good God is, to give me the joy of seeing that place, the only one where he was always well received. I think the Clarist convent is the only place from which it can be seen from here. I have been here for twelve days, and am even more alone and hidden than at Nazareth. I am not living at the convent as a servant—there is a Negro who does the errands in the town and an altar boy to serve the Masses.

I am like a *workman* living on his labor at the door of the convent. This suits me better because there is more solitude and silence, and it is even more like the hidden life of our Lord. Inwardly, my life is as it was, and outwardly I follow the Benedictine time-table for hours of work, prayer, rising and so on, doing what you told me, *fac hoc et vives*.[61] I work the hours the rule prescribes, and it is long enough, I think, to earn my living. I have been given work I can do in my cell, and which I think is of service to the convent: making holy pictures, which are greatly needed in the convent.

The Abbess is very different in character from the one at Nazareth (whose spiritual superior she is) but resembles her in her goodness towards me. The other one showed herself a sister to

[60] Cf. Luke 10:42.
[61] "Do this, and thou shalt live."

me, this one is a mother. The other one was a very great soul, this one is a saint. She possesses in the highest degree what, nine years ago, you used to admire in St. Teresa: *a head of ice and a heart of fire*, with that indomitable *strength of character* which alone makes it possible to undertake and perform everything for and with God. It is the same thing as we admire and love in my dear cousin, who is no doubt now near you in Paris, and to whom all my thoughts constantly return, as they do to you, dear father.

There is one thing that reminds me especially of both you and her in this month of October. It was on one of the last days of October—the 29th or 30th, about the date you will receive this letter—twelve years ago that I appeared for the first time at your confessional, when you brought me back to God and sent me to Communion and became my father. Pray hard for me at this time when I am so near you, and so full of emotion. Thank you, dear father—what have you not been to me since then? How much I needed God to give me you as my father, and how good he was to give me such a gift! How blessed I am in it! And your task with me is not over yet, for I have some serious things to ask you. My letter is already a long one, and it is hardly begun yet.

The day before yesterday the good Abbess had me called to the parlor.

"We should like to make you a somewhat longer tunic with a hood for the winter and constant wear, something like that worn by the country people here—something which while both a little more conservative and appropriate to the religious life than your trousers and blue linen smock, will still not be of the same color as that worn by any of the religious orders."

Myself: "I am a Frenchman and not a Syrian; on me it would still be either a disguise (which is not important) or a religious habit—a hermit's habit if you like, but in the last resort a religious habit, which I could wear only with the bishop's permission. By doing so, I should not lose my *poverty*, but I should lose my *humble status*. I should no longer be preaching Jesus, the workman of Nazareth, so loudly from the rooftops, and I should no longer be singing so clearly the beautiful song of his divine abjection."

The Abbess: "Well, then, ask your director what he thinks of my wish."

Myself: "Very well, I'll ask him."

The Abbess: "And now—why are you not a priest?"

Myself: "First because I chose to leave my Order; next, because I wanted to stay in the lowest place; and lastly, it is impossible because I have nothing to live on."

The Abbess: "You would be imitating Jesus just as well as you are now—you would be practising his poverty just the same, following him in his public life instead of his hidden life. Even your abjection would be no less. Instead of finding it where he did, at Nazareth, in the obscurity and lowliness of life of a workman, you would find it as he did in preaching—in contradiction, difficulties, setbacks, calumnies and persecution. As for the question of means of livelihood, I am astonished to hear you mention it. I will offer you a position as our chaplain, either in our convent here or in the one at Nazareth, whichever you chose, for as long as you live—the sooner the better; we should be very happy if it could be within a year. What I foresee for you, is not merely that you should be our chaplain—I am offering you that as a means to an end, so that you can ask for ordination to the priesthood in order to become our chaplain. Keep the post as long as you wish and while you fill it, make disciples among us, in the shadow of our cloisters—men like yourself. And when there are enough of them, when the right moment comes, go with them wherever the Holy Spirit guides you. If you are going to have disciples, it would be better in any case to be a priest yourself when you come to train them."

Myself: "One has to be called by God for that. One has to have a mission. I cannot give it to myself. Jesus left his life as a workman to go as a laborer in the Gospel—but only when his hour had come. There is nothing to show me that mine will ever come, and that I shall ever be anything but what I am now. On the contrary, I feel immeasurably weak und unworthy. To offer the Holy Sacrifice seems like a dream to me, so unworthy of it do I feel. And the direction of souls seems the one thing in the world I am least capable of doing. Besides, my way of life suits me: here I am able to sing the beautiful song of the poverty and abjection of Jesus."

The Abbess: "You would not be singing it any the less, any more than Jesus sang it less clearly at Capharnaum than at Nazareth—and besides, you would be teaching others to sing it. We must do something for our neighbors. God does not need men, but because it has pleased him to make use of them, we must serve him in this way. And it would seem the time has come: you are forty years old. You feel incapable—and that is just as it should be. Besides, if one waited till one were capable before acting, one would never act. Talk about it to your director. We shall pray for you, that Jesus will inspire this longing in you. I am convinced that the Patriarch will help you: his heart is in the right place."

So there it is! You must decide everything once and for all. "He that heareth you, heareth me" . . . Is there anything good in the depths of my soul? Certainly, *by no will of my own,* there is a secret longing in me to found a religious congregation—and I have said nothing about it to anyone but you. I envisage the rule of St. Benedict . . . practised *in the spirit of St. Benedict,* and for that reason following his rule in many points, but not in all. That is the life I should have offered Brother Pierre if he had chosen to follow me, and it is the one I practise. It is little less austere than the ancient rule of La Trappe, but considerably more so than the present one. It is much simpler than either of them. It is largely relieved of the multitude of vocal prayers that weighs them down, and there is much more in it about poverty and work. "You are truly monks when you live by the labor of your hands, like our fathers and the apostles," the rule of St. Benedict says.[62] I visualize a big reduction in exterior ceremonies, so that— as among the ancient monks—a great deal of time is left for mental prayer and the interior life, and also for practising *charity towards our neighbor at every opportunity God affords*— in short, "loving God and one's neighbor."

The *concealed, quiet, latent* longing to see this truly Benedictine way of life established through the medium of a foundation in the Holy Land, and actually to help re-establish it, is certainly in my mind, though by no conscious will of mine. With it is profound submission to the will of God: I am equally ready never to see it realized or to do what would be pleasing to God to bring about its fulfillment. It will be clear that the very generous, affectionate and maternal suggestion made by this holy soul [the Abbess] is in perfect harmony with my *secret* longing, of which she knew nothing. She is making possible what had seemed impossible —she is suddenly putting into my hands *all* the necessary means, means which have seemed so far beyond my reach.

It is also quite true that by doing what she suggests, I shall not be following our Lord any less closely, for my poverty will be no less, nor my abjection—and I shall meet with contradiction, opposition, calumnies and persecution, especially in the poor Holy Land I love and which is not a charitable place (though that only makes me want to work all the more for the establishment of its reign here, as far as my nothingness allows).

As for *firm resolves,* I am aware of only one in me: not to allow

[62] The Rule of St. Benedict, section 148.

myself to be turned aside either from the imitation of our Lord or from obedience to him. I am already following him, and by doing what the good Abbess suggests I should not be doing so any less perfectly. I also have obedience, inasmuch as I obey you. "He who heareth you, heareth me." So then, the whole matter is for you to decide by showing me the will of God for me: whether I ought to stay as I am, or should accept the good Mother's suggestion. In any case, it seems to me that if I stay as I am, I ought also—following Jesus' example—to keep the blessed clothing of a workman, which is what he wore at Nazareth. The question of changing my dress arises only if you decide I ought one day to accept Holy Orders. In that case I should want to change my beloved smock, not for some kind of semi-religious and fantastic clothing, but for the Benedictine habit which any bishop will allow anyone to wear, because anyone may profess the Benedictine rule without joining any of the numerous existing Benedictine congregations. Thus a change of dress would be a serious matter, equivalent to religious profession; I would make it as and when you might wish, but in any case I think before receiving Minor Orders, or at that time.

I should be quite happy were you to tell me to stay as I am; and very happy, too, if you were to tell me otherwise, although I am scared by the prospect of the innumerable crosses I foresee in taking another course, and am as it were crushed beneath the weight of my powerlessness and incapacity, which are blindingly obvious to me, and throw me down like St. Paul on the way to Damascus. "He who heareth you, heareth me."

Whatever you decide, I shall accept it with joy, gratitude and benediction, and shall follow it out literally, with all my heart.

After all, if I do not want to know the will of our Beloved and do it, what do I want? "He who heareth you, heareth him." Speak then, my most dear father, and you will be joyfully obeyed, although the possibility of changing my condition frightens me. Now all I have is pleasant, but in a change I foresee nothing but crosses. These egotistic reflections will prove to you how cowardly I am. I am blushing at the thought that they will tell you how little I am worth. I have let my pen run on—but at least my letters to you do show you my soul stripped quite naked.

Tell me about yourself, dear father, and about your health. Have you been able to go on saying Mass? Tell me about my cousin who is my mother as you are my father. I wrote to her today without saying a word to her (any more than I have to anyone else) about what I have told you. But you can tell her anything you like about me. Give me, please, the advice I need. Carry me like the Good Shepherd, as a father does his infant child.

Pray for me. I love and venerate you with all my heart in the heart of our beloved Jesus.

Your child in Jesus,

Brother Charles [63]

Jerusalem, October 22, 1898

My beloved father:

I want to say two things about my letter of a week ago.

1. The deeper I dig into my soul, the more clearly I see there only one desire: to do what God wants of me, whatever it may be—what will be most pleasing to him, what will best give glory to him, what holds the most love, what will lead me to love him best. To give as much glory as I can to him, and in order to do so, to love him as much as I can; and to do what will lead me to him.

As far as I am concerned, that is everything. So then, choose for me what holds the most love, what will make me most loving,

[63] Cf. C, pp. 87–95.

the most acceptable thing I can do for our only Beloved. You know me: put this child in the place where Jesus would be most pleased for me to be.

2. When I told you I wanted to take the Benedictine habit and had a secret longing to form a little Benedictine community in the Holy Land if God would send the souls, I expressed myself badly—I ought to have said a *monastic* habit and a *monastic* community. Although in shaping my own day I follow the Benedictine rule, I should not like to adopt either the Benedictine habit or the Benedictine rule as such. I venerate and admire them. But on the one hand the rule was made for big communities and not for "little flocks," and on the other—and more important—to adopt it would be to precipitate myself back into those discussions about the interpretation of texts and the spirit and the letter, in which one can drown, and which lead good souls to spend their time thinking about unimportant nothings instead of using it to love God.

What I secretly dream of, without confessing or admitting it even to myself, even indeed, trying to expel it, for it is constantly recurring (and I am admitting it to you because you ought to know the lowest depths of my soul), what I involuntarily dream of is something very simple and numerically small, resembling the simple communities of the Church's early days. A few souls united to lead the life of Nazareth, living like the Holy Family by their own labor and practising the Nazarene virtues in contemplating Jesus—a little family, a little *monastic* home, quite small and simple, and certainly not Benedictine.

I am delightfully placed as an insignificant workman hidden away in St. Clare's shadow. I have found what I was looking for to perfection, wonderfully. I really lead the life of our Lord at Nazareth, and I shall be quite happy to stay as I am until my death, as long as it is not the will of God that I should change.

If God's will is that I should be the chaplain to the good nuns, I am ready to obey, and to be so until my death, if he so wills. I am sure that by doing so I should not be ceasing to imitate him. I should still be in his divine poverty, and should be changing the lowliness of the workman of Nazareth for the tribulations and crosses of the worker for the Gospel. There would be less solitude—but more works of charity.

If later our Lord chooses to send me a few souls to live the life of Nazareth in one of the deserts of the Holy Land where he walked and preached the Gospel in former times, to live with the contemplation, work, hospitality, charity and simplicity of the primitive ages, I am ready to obey. I should equally be following our Lord; crosses and conflict would replace the worker's obscurity —as they did for him; there would be less complete withdrawal, but more acts of charity. I am in your hands, wanting only one thing, to glorify our beloved Jesus as much as I can. Do for your child what in the light of his presence seems to you most pleasing to his Heart.

My interior life is very simple. It is made up entirely of a series of brief spiritual communions at very short intervals—it is very consoling.

I find long mental prayer before the Blessed Sacrament very difficult. I am in a strange state. Everything seems to be empty, empty, hollow, immeasurably insignificant, except only being at our Lord's feet and gazing on him—but when I am at his feet I am dry, arid, with neither words nor thoughts—and frequently, alas, in the end I fall asleep.

I make myself read, but everything seems hollow to me. I am reading St. Thomas' *Summa Theologica.* The contents of the sisters' library (less full than that at Nazareth) are such that scarcely anything except the *Summa* and St. Francis de Sales attracts me. Should I go on with this reading? I am told that some books have arrived for me at Nazareth. They will send them when they have an opportunity. Would they be books on theology sent by you? If they are, thank you. I will thank you again when I have them. . . .[64]

Brother Charles expressed the same thoughts in the text which follows:

October 15, 1898, Feast of St. Teresa

O dear mother, St. Teresa, how much I need you! How much I need you to fashion my interior life! Have I ever had one? I do not know—but certainly at this moment I have none. Used there to be anything in the garden of my soul? I do not know, but at this moment everything in it is dried up, ruined, torn out. One might say with the Psalmist that a beast, a "boar out of the wood hath laid it waste." Was it the devil? Did I do it myself, by allowing him to mislead me? Did I do it by my own negligence? St. Teresa, strengthen and enlighten me, I am asking only one thing of you, and you know what it is. I want only one thing: to give glory to our Lord Jesus as far as I am able, and, in order to do so, to love him as much as I can. That is what I am asking of you, dearest mother; give me both it and everything necessary to it. No, I am not asking for consolation, or anything except this one thing: that I may glorify our Lord as much as is possible to me, and that to do so, I may do his will. Loving him as much as possible, loving him as much as I can—both come down to doing his will always (for he does not refuse to make it known to those who love him as much as they can, and seek ardently—as is proper to such love—to learn the will of the Beloved, so as to be able to do it).

Dear mother, help me, come help me! You who loved so much to imitate your Spouse, imitate him now when he said:

[64] Cf. C, pp. 96–9.

"Him that cometh to me I will not cast out." Hear my prayer, pray, pray for me, that today and forever I may glorify our Lord as much as possible and, to do so, may love him as much as possible.

Remember, it is one of our Lord's brothers who is calling to you for help, and remember what your Spouse said to you about those Sisters of the Incarnation when you hesitated about helping them. Do not therefore hesitate now. See my soul, battered and ravaged, and help me, good mother, for the love of Jesus your Spouse. I think you have heard me and will help me—you already brought me one great grace in the past year, for which I thank you with all my heart.

I think it is to you too that I should attribute the benefit of having read this year the books of your son, St. John of the Cross. Thank you a thousand times for that, too, beloved mother. It is you who by the will of God inspire me to turn to you today and lay before you the poor garden of my soul, which is in such a lamentable condition. I think you are already replying very quietly in a phrase which I must make the key to everything, the rule by which I cultivate the garden of my soul, with Jesus' help and yours: the phrase "the most perfect," and that always in perfect obedience to my spiritual director: "He that heareth you, heareth me." I must be most perfect in all the day's tasks, doing them most perfectly. I must be most perfect in doing everything "as the Lord Jesus would have done it in my place." [65]

The years 1899 and 1900 were years spent in seeking, during which Brother Charles was asking God in which direction he wanted him to go. It was night for him, and a very dark night, but he went on quietly searching, daily putting himself into the hands of God.

The following extracts are from letters written at that time:

[65] From "Short Meditations on the Feasts of Every Day of the Year" (1897–1898; cf. OS, p. 319 ff.).

To his sister, Marie de Blic:

Nazareth, May 8, 1899

Bona crux. It is through the cross that we achieve union with him who was nailed there, our heavenly Spouse. We should accept, as we would a favor, every moment of our lives and whatever they may bring, whether it is good or bad, but the crosses with even greater gratitude than the rest. Crosses release us from this world and by doing so bind us to God.[66]

Nazareth, July 21, 1899

We should attach no importance either to the events of this life or to material things: they are the dreams of a night spent at an inn, and will vanish as quickly as images seen in dreams, leaving no more traces than they do. What will remain at the hour of our death, except our merits and sins? We must see things as they are, in the great light of the faith which illumines our thoughts with daylight so bright that we see things with an eye very different from that of poor souls tied to the world. Like faith itself, the habit of seeing things in the light of faith raises us above the mists and mud of this world. It puts us into a new atmosphere, in full sunshine, full daylight, in a serene calm and luminous peace far above the region of clouds, winds and storms, beyond the realm of twilight and night.

At every moment of our lives, in time and in eternity, we must live by faith, believing in what grace leads us to hope for, expecting to possess it in glory, loving him who will be "our infinite reward." [67]

Nazareth, October 13, 1899

Thank you for your good wishes on my birthday. Yes, I was

[66] Cf. ES, p. 189.
[67] *Ibid.*

pleased to be forty-one, for I am happy to watch the dissolution of my body and the end of my pilgrimage coming nearer.

I am very well, but I am conscious of the prophet's voice saying: *"All flesh is grass and the glory thereof (passes) as the flower of the field: in the morning, it flourishes, in the evening, it is withered, because the spirit of the Lord hath blown upon it."* [68]

I give praises to God for giving you another child, another soul, another saint: what joy and honor for you! Under the protection of what inhabitant of heaven shall you put this blessed child?

Yes, my dear, I am praying for you, and shall do more and more. Above all else, do not torture yourself—do not worry. Yes, live simply, avoid any unnecessary expense; in your manner and way of life, withdraw ever further from everything that smacks of the world, vanity and pride. These are follies which serve only to diminish our future glory in heaven and prolong our purgatory, burdening us with the responsibility of having given an unhealthy example to others, fixing us in a way of doing things condemned by natural reason and rejected even more firmly by the Christian religion, and which a sensible person could adopt only for the sake of being like other people, when it would be much better to give them a good example than to imitate their madness. Yes indeed, do away with all futility and everything that smacks of the world. But do not torture yourself; do not be afraid of the future.

Overlook nothing, absolutely nothing, that could contribute to the good moral and intellectual development of your children, nor anything that might be of value in your own interior spiritual progress. There must be no economizing on good books. If souls consecrated to God, monks who think about perfection from morning till night, feel the need right to the end of their lives

[68] Cf. Is. 40: 6 ff. and Ps. 89:6 ff.

to read and reread the works of the masters of the spiritual life and the lives of the saints who have gone before them, how much more must they need it who live in the world, in the middle of so many distracting occupations? There must be no economizing on alms; no reductions here, but rather increases: "Give . . . and it shall be given to you . . . with the same measure that you mete it shall be measured to you . . . what you give to the poor, you give to me."

The best way to lack nothing is always to share very generously with the poor, seeing in them Jesus' representatives and Jesus himself.

Then again, trust. "He who gives life will also give food; he who has given the body will surely also give clothing. Seek the kingdom of God and his justice (that is, perfection) and all these things shall be added unto you." These words were said to all Christians, and not only to monks.

Trust, trust! Be free from all anxiety. Bring up your children well for God's sake, and God will arrange their future a hundred thousand times better than you or all the people in the world put together, could do.[69]

To his Trappist friend, Father Jerome:

Nazareth, January 28, 1900

My very dear father and good brother in Jesus:

We are still in the Christmas season. Physically I am at Nazareth, but in spirit I have been at Bethlehem for more than a month now. Thus it is from beside the manger, between Mary and Joseph, that I am writing to you. How good it is here! Outside there is cold and snow, symbols of the world, but how good it

[69] Cf. ES, pp. 192–4.

is to be here, in this little cave, lit by the light of Jesus. How pleasant, warm and bright it is. Our good dear Father Abbot wants to know what it is the gentle Infant Jesus has been whispering to me for the past month while I have been gazing at him, keeping watch at his feet by night with his holy parents, taking him into my arms and to my breast, taking him into my heart at Holy Communion. He is continually repeating: "The Will of God—the Will of God." "Behold, I come: in the head of the book it is written of me that I should do thy will."

The will of God, and the will of God by the path of obedience: that is what the beloved voice of the divine Infant Jesus, gently murmuring, keeps saying to me.[70]

Nazareth, March 8, 1900

How good it is to empty one's mind of all visible things to fill it only with the hope of heavenly things! And how fortunate we are even here below! Of course there are unpleasant things, our sins especially, and with them the long train of our imperfections and weaknesses, but when we remember that our Beloved Jesus is always in our souls, when we see the divine Host, what can we say except that the darkness has gone out of the night of our lives: *Nox illuminatio mea in deliciis meis?* [71] This poor world that was so dark is transformed into delightful radiance by the light streaming from the divine victim, "the light of the world unto the consummation of the ages." Though not for everyone, for, alas, many are still in the shadow of death. But for us, the privileged, as a special gift to us, we who "have been chosen, and did not first choose." Ah, dear brother in Jesus, how fortunate we are!

---

[70] Cf. ES, p. 195.
[71] Cf. Ps. 138:11: "Night shall be my light in my pleasures."

Tell me how you are. I shall not worry if your health is bad: life or death, health or sickness are God's business and not ours. What he gives us in this respect is always what is best for us. All we have to do is rejoice at it always, always. . . .[72]

In April 1900, events began to move quickly and plans began to become more definite. On April 26 he wrote a long letter to his director, the Abbé Huvelin.

My beloved father:

Yesterday something so important happened, not in the world of external events, but in my thoughts, that I believe I ought to tell you about it. With your agreement, if you will give it me, I am going to work (as you already know) for two things: to bring the Mount of the Beatitudes into the hands of the Church by giving it into the keeping of the Franciscans [73] and to see set up there as soon as possible a tabernacle and an altar, no matter how plain, where our Lord may dwell and daily Mass be said in perpetuity. Now, it is very clear to me that the Franciscans are ready to promise to do it in the future, an indeterminate future, but not at this present moment. I was thinking of offering them to lay the burden of the cost on me. I could maintain a Maronite priest there, thanks to a small income made available by my family. But I am now convinced that *I simply cannot let this burden fall on my family.* As it is, I shall already have to turn to them when it comes to setting up the altar, however poor it may be. There is only one thing left to do: become the poverty-ridden chaplain myself.

I saw this very clearly yesterday, on the Feast of St. Mark.

---

[72] Cf. ES, p. 195 ff.

[73] Brother Charles had learned that the property was for sale. Cf. Carrouges, *Soldier of the Spirit: The Life of Charles de Foucauld,* p. 146.

And as today is the Feast of our Lady of Good Counsel, it seemed to me that by putting myself under her protection, I could and should profit from a feast so propitious for making a choice and taking a stand in so grave a matter, although of course *leaving everything to your judgement.* "He who heareth you, heareth me." I obtained permission to spend the night before the Blessed Sacrament, and there, praying my hardest to my good Mother, the holy Virgin, I slowly came to a decision, which I will summarize for you.

My vocation is to imitate as perfectly as possible *our Lord's hidden life at Nazareth.* Should I reach this goal more certainly by receiving Holy Orders and setting myself up as a hermit-priest on the deserted summit of the Mount of the Beatitudes, or by staying as I am? To answer this question, I looked closely at the chief virtues I have to practise in the imitation of our Lord in his hidden life.

1. *Faith.* There, on the Mount of the Beatitudes, isolated and alone in the middle of ill-disposed Arabs, I should have greater need of faith than here, where I am safe and in the midst of plenty.

2. *Chastity.* Alone there, I shall be much better off than here. That goes without saying.

3. *Love of my neighbor.* There, in prayer I shall do infinitely more for my neighbor simply by offering the Holy Sacrifice. Through works there, too, I shall do much more for him, whether it be by the setting up of a tabernacle which, by the very presence of the Blessed Sacrament silently sanctifies the district around; or whether it be by pilgrimages, sources of prayer and graces brought into being there; or again by hospitality, alms and the good I shall try to do there. Here, there is nothing of all that.

4. *Poverty.* It will be infinitely greater there, for I shall be without everything. Here I have everything in abundance.

5. *Humility.* In my present position, I am more lowly. But

where would I be imitating our Lord the more closely? No man ever follows our Lord more perfectly than by offering the Holy Sacrifice or administering the sacraments. Therefore it cannot be good to seek for a kind of humility which takes one away from the priesthood, because it also takes one away from the imitation of our Lord who is "the only way." It would therefore be wrong for me to keep myself in the greater lowliness of my present position, or to be so afraid of the elevation of the priesthood as to reject it; *I should see humility where our Lord saw it, practise it as he practised it, and thus practise it in the priesthood, following his example.*

I am cutting this down so as not to tire you. Having looked at prayer, love of truth, abjection, penance, courage, obedience to God, the pure search for what is good in God's eyes (withdrawal, love of God, the imitation of our Lord, and hope, all from this point of view), I have come to the conclusion that it would be better for me to be there than here. Especially would this be true as there I shall be quite abandoned in the middle of all kinds of difficulties, really carrying Jesus' cross and sharing his poverty, and also because I shall be in infinitely greater solitude and would be able to do good works that are quite impossible to me here and—underlying everything else—because there is nothing that gives as much glory to God in this world as the presence and offering of the Holy Eucharist. By the mere fact of celebrating the holy Mass and setting up a tabernacle, I shall be giving the greatest glory to God and doing most good to men. The outcome of my "election," which was very long and complicated, indicated clearly that from my point of view, to fulfill my special vocation— *the imitation of our Lord in his hidden life*—in the most perfect way I should go to become a priest-hermit on the Mount of the Beatitudes.

But then there was something else to be decided.

How and when should I do it?

First I should tell you that I still dream constantly of the monastic life. What came out of my Holy Week was the conclusion that I should leave the Convent of St. Clare where I am (forgive the expression) "cock of the walk," and become a hermit in some other field, on the hills overlooking Nazareth, carrying *Jesus' cross in poverty and hard work* there. At that time I had no thought of the Mount of the Beatitudes, nor yet of the priesthood. But suddenly all three things coalesced, amalgamated and began to look to me as some kind of necessity. I have not written to you about this earlier, so as not to confuse things: we already have the questions of the poor widow and buying the Mount of the Beatitudes. Though according to what I last heard, the good widow will not need me any longer.

What then should I do? I *leave the decision entirely to you,* dear father: "I put my soul in your hands." I shall do what you decide. But for my part, I think I should send you by an early post a report on the rule of life I drew up eighteen months ago [74] and have been following ever since (apart from the habit, and as far as one can do alone), asking you to obtain permission for me to take the habit in accordance with it from Cardinal Richard whom I think I can regard as my Bishop (having lived so long in Paris, domiciled there, and having been a *vagus* everywhere else both before and since, and having kept up no connection with Strasbourg where I was born). Obtain for me from Cardinal Richard permission to become a hermit according to this rule and to live according to it (there can be no question of any but annual vows, and even if there were several of us, the congregation would be quite small), and ask him, too, for the favor of permission for us to be ordained as missionary hermits. My little rule of the Hermits of the Sacred Heart of Jesus has been drawn up ex-

[74] On January 6, 1899.

pressly to make it possible for several persons to live without indiscipline the life of a small family unit with a triple aim: to lead a life following the pattern of our Lord's hidden life at Nazareth; to practice (as soon as there are a sufficient number) perpetual adoration of the Blessed Sacrament exposed; and to live among pagans in mission countries.

I began this rule twenty months ago, when I was in Armenia, trying to bring back that young man.[75] Since then I have completed and observed it. As soon as you have obtained this triple favor for me from the Cardinal, and the purchase of the Mount of the Beatitudes is an accomplished fact (once the money is here, that will not take longer than two months), I shall leave for Our Lady of the Snows. There I shall be given excellent training as a priest by the good Father Abbot, who is the brother of the Abbot of Staouëli, and with whom I have maintained the friendliest of relations. At the same time, I shall come to see you, my beloved father, because as you will understand at this solemn moment I need more than ever your blessing and counsel. Then, when you think fit, I shall receive Holy Orders, and immediately afterwards I shall leave for the Holy Land.

I must add, however, that although so sacred a thing as training for the priesthood must be afforded the necessary time, in this case we ought to move quite quickly. *A hermit ought to stay in the desert* like a fish in water. I ought not to extend my stay either with the Trappists or elsewhere. My place is at the hermitage in the desert. *Force of necessity* alone has decided me to make this journey: it is the only way I can see of being sure to have a good priestly training. At the same time—I praise God for it—it will bring me to your feet. Perhaps God will give me a companion while I am in France. But I must not stay away from the

[75] Brother Pierre (the journey was to Alexandretta and Akbès in September 1898. See pp. 116–17 and Carrouges, *op. cit.* p. 143).

Holy Land, the desert and my hermitage any longer than is absolutely necessary. If I receive the money from my brother-in-law in a month or a month and a half, and if you get this threefold favor for me from the Cardinal, I should perhaps be able to arrive in France in August or September of this year. In this matter as in every other, I will do *as you wish and what you wish.* But so as to be ready myself and so as not to delay by any fault of my own the earliest possible foundation of the shrine so dear to my heart, I am going from now on to do as much as I can towards reviving my theology, and to start saying the breviary again.

If your decision is that I should stay as I am, I shall relinquish it all again without any dismay. For, beloved father, wholly sinful and unworthy as I am, I want only what God wills, and I know that whatever he may ordain, I shall rejoice in it with all my heart. I do, it is true, feel some regret at leaving the pleasant and tranquil life at St. Clare's—and I feel it even more strongly at giving up the profound abjection of my blue smock. I am also somewhat apprehensive and as it were dizzy at the thought of the isolation, nakedness and difficulties in the midst of which I shall find myself on that deserted mountain peak. It looks to me as though I were throwing myself into the sea, like St. Peter. I also feel redoubled affection for the good nuns who have made my life so pleasant that in their house I have not been able to feel Jesus' cross. But in spite of all that, I still want, if it is the will of God, to go and establish myself up there and to be a priest and hermit, for I believe that by doing so I shall be giving great glory to him, even if I am always alone, though that glory would be even greater should he send me some companions.

Otherwise, I am enjoying profound peace, conscious of real joy in everything that is happening, because everything is either willed or permitted by God, and nothing can hurt me. I believe that I long to do the will of God with my whole heart, and that I shall find joy in doing everything he ordains, whatever it may be.

So then, beloved father, whatever your reply to me may be, whatever you say to me, I hope, with the help of God's grace, to find great joy in it. I may ask him for that, for I want always to enjoy doing his will. I beg you to give me the news about your health—do not forget!

Kneeling at your feet, beloved father, I beseech you to bless your child, all unworthy and worthless as he is. He venerates and loves you with all his heart in the Sacred Heart of our beloved Jesus.

Brother Charles of Jesus [76]

[76] Cf. C, pp. 133–40.

PART THREE

*From Ordination (June 9, 1901)
to Death (December 1, 1916)*

*O*n *August 16, 1900 Charles de Foucauld landed at Mar-*
seilles. On August 14, 1901, he wrote to his friend Henry de
Castries, "It is just a year ago that on my confessor's advice I
took the road back to France to receive Holy Orders there."

Brother Charles of Jesus reached Our Lady of the Snows on
September 29, 1900. He was delighted to find himself living in a
cell which opened onto the chapel.

Brother Charles of Jesus spent the whole of the last night of the
year 1900 in adoration before the Blessed Sacrament. At Our
Lady of the Snows he led a life of unbroken contemplation. He
was ordained deacon on March 23, the day before Passion Sun-
day. On May 9, he began a month of retreat in preparation for
ordination to the priesthood. Some time later, he wrote:

I am an old sinner who since almost immediately after his
conversion, nearly twenty years ago, has been powerfully drawn
by Jesus to lead his life at Nazareth. Since that time I have
been struggling to imitate him—though, alas, very poorly—and I
spent several years in dear, blessed Nazareth as servant and sacristan to a Convent of Poor Clares. The only reason why I left that
blessed place five years ago was to receive Holy Orders. I am
now an unattached priest of the diocese of Viviers, my final
retreats before ordination to the diaconate and priesthood having
shown me that the life of Nazareth, which was my vocation, ought
to be led not in the Holy Land I love so much, but among the

most distressed souls, the sheep most completely lost. The divine feast of which I am the minister must be offered not to the brethren and their relations and the rich neighbors, but to the lamest and blindest of men, the most abandoned souls, those without priests. When I was young, I traveled through Algeria and Morocco. Morocco is as big as France and has ten million inhabitants, but there is not a single priest in the interior. In the Algerian Sahara, which is seven or eight times the size of France and with a population greater than was formerly thought, there are a dozen missionaries. It seemed to me that there was no more abandoned race than these and I asked and obtained the permission of the Most Reverend Apostolic Prefect of the Sahara to settle in the Algerian Sahara and lead there either alone or with a few priests or laymen, brothers in Jesus, a life as close as possible to the hidden life of our beloved Jesus at Nazareth. . . .[1]

Charles de Foucauld chose his path during the retreat before his ordination to the priesthood:

Quis? (who?) One whose duty it is to follow Jesus, imitating him, the Saviour, the Good Shepherd, who came "to bring fire to the earth" and "to save what was lost."

Ubi? (where?) Wherever is most perfect. Not where humanly speaking there would be the most opportunities to pick up novices, ecclesiastical authorizations, money, lands or support, but wherever is most perfect in itself, most perfect in Jesus' sense of the words, most in conformity with the perfection of the Gospels, most in conformity with the inspiration of the Holy Spirit; the places where Jesus would go, where the sheep have strayed farthest, to the most diseased of Jesus' brethren, the most abandoned, those who have the fewest shepherds, those sitting in the densest darkness, the deepest shadow of death; to those most

[1] From a letter, dated April 8, 1905 to Abbé Caron (cf. ES, pp. 203 ff.).

tightly bound by the devil, the most blind, the most completely lost. And primarily to the unbelieving Mohammedans and pagans of Morocco and the surrounding countries of North Africa.

Quibus auxiliis? (with whose help?) Jesus' alone, for "seek ye first the kingdom of God and his justice, and all these things shall be added unto you"; and "if you dwell in me and my words dwell in you, all that you ask shall be done." Jesus gave no special powers to his apostles; if I do their works, I shall have their graces.

Cur? (why?) Because this is how I can give most glory to Jesus, love him, obey him and imitate him best. The Gospel, my own yearnings and my director are all urging me in this direction. Why? To make Jesus, the Sacred Heart and the Blessed Virgin known to the brethren of Jesus who do not know him; to feed with the Holy Eucharist the brothers of Jesus who have never tasted it; to baptize the brothers of Jesus still held slaves by the devil; to teach the Gospel, the story of Jesus, the evangelical virtues, and the sweetness of the maternal breast of his Church to the brothers of Jesus who have never heard of them.

Quando? (when?) "Mary rising up . . . went into the hill country with haste": when one is full of Jesus, one is also full of charity. Therefore it will be as soon as I am reasonably prepared and my director is inspired by the Spirit of God to say: "Go!"

Would it not be better to go to the Holy Land first? *No.* One soul is worth more than the whole of the Holy Land and all things created without the gift of reason put together. It is a question of going, not where the land is most holy, but where souls are in the greatest need.

Is not the whole of this exercise in election a temptation arising from self-love and pride? No, because its result in this life will be neither consolation nor honor, but many crosses and humiliations: "Whether you are despised for it, or I am glorified, in either case you will be rewarded" (our Lord to St. Teresa).

What proof is there that my choice here expresses the will of

God? The two sayings of Jesus: "Follow me," and "When thou makest a dinner or a supper, call not thy friends, nor thy brethren, nor thy kinsmen nor thy neighbors who are rich . . . But when thou makest a feast, call the poor, the maimed, the lame and the blind" (Luke 14:12–13).[2]

Brother Charles was ordained priest on June 9.

On June 23 he wrote to his friend Henry de Castries, the explorer, and told him of his longing to found a hermitage on the frontier of Morocco.

Brother Charles of Jesus left Our Lady of the Snows on September 6, 1901. He arrived in Algiers on the 10th. Monseigneur Guérin was expecting him and told him he could settle as a monk at Beni-Abbès. Brother Charles of Jesus was to administer the sacraments to the soldiers of this oasis on the Moroccan frontier, but what he wanted "above all" to do was "all the good possible at this moment in time for the Moslem population, who are so numerous and so deserted, by taking Jesus in the Most Blessed Sacrament among them, as the Blessed Virgin sanctified John the Baptist by carrying Jesus to him."

He left Algiers on October 15. From Ain-Sefra he traveled by short stages on horseback to Beni-Abbès. On the journey he said Mass at Taghit: "I find it so moving to bring Jesus down into these places he probably never visited in the flesh."

He celebrated the first Mass at Beni-Abbès on October 29, 1901. Then he set himself to work building his hermitage, the Fraternity of the Sacred Heart. The chapel was completed on November 30, and he celebrated Mass there for the first time on the December 1, fifteen years to the day before his death.

On April 28, 1902 he wrote to his cousin:

[2] Cf. ES, pp. 205 ff.

I have been granted permission to found a new religious family under the Rule of St. Augustine with the name "The Little Brothers of the Most Sacred Heart of Jesus." Its task is to pray day and night before the Blessed Sacrament exposed, in solitude, within the monastic enclosure, living in poverty and by work in mission countries.[3]

In November 1902 he wrote from Beni-Abbès to his friend Henry de Castries:

I am very, very happy. The distant echoes of the sorrows of the world reaching me here lead me to turn my gaze with a greater joy to our maternal home, the Church, the Bride of Christ, who is growing ever younger and more beautiful, and towards that heavenly fatherland where "we shall be like God, for we shall see him as he is." Of course, one would like to see souls believing and loving, to see the nations now sitting in the shadow of death open their eyes to the great light, and to see the reign of good. But the wretched state of created things cannot blot out the profound joy in my soul, the "influx of peace" born of the thought of the infinite, vast, immutable beatitude of the Creator. We must "give thanks to him for his great glory," rejoicing that he is God.[4]

After a year at Beni-Abbès, Brother Charles of Jesus took stock:

Beni-Abbès, December 15, 1902

My beloved father:

Another year almost gone, another step towards eternity. With

[3] From a letter to Madame de Bondy (cf. TPF, p. 133).
[4] From a letter dated November 5, 1902 (cf. LHC, p. 134).

all my heart I shall be with you at Christmas and New Year, beseeching Jesus to give you the only necessary and desirable gift: that of being and doing what will please him most at every moment of your life. I ask him for this every day at Mass and Benediction of the Blessed Sacrament. But during these holy and blessed days I shall ask him for it even more than usual, while the Infant Jesus is in his manger and graciously gives himself into my hands. . . .

My life is still following the same course. Outwardly I am very busy, although very calm: every day the same, always the poor and the sick. Inwardly, I have to reproach myself with not giving enough time to prayer and purely spiritual things. During the day there is always someone knocking at my door, and at night, which should be a propitious time, I am wretch enough to sleep. That sleep is taking up more time than I might wish and is a shame and torment to me. I have not the time for it, and yet it takes it.

I am *very well:* in perfect health since my brief overtiredness in the autumn.

My examination of conscience leads me to reproach myself with three things chiefly: *lukewarmness towards Jesus*—I pray neither as much nor as lovingly as I could and should; *lukewarmness towards my neighbor*—I do not see Jesus clearly enough in my neighbor, and I do not love him as myself; and *lukewarmness towards the cross*—I do not seek suffering, I am slothful and I eat too much. This examination of conscience is certainly not complete, but these are the chief things both at the moment and for the whole year 1902.

For some time now, and more strongly every day, I cannot turn my thoughts away from Morocco, with its ten million inhabitants, all unbelievers, a not inconsiderable but wholly abandoned nation. There is neither priest nor missionary there. In the ports where there are Spanish consulates there are consulate chaplains, but that is all. In the interior, in a land as big as France, there is not an altar, a priest or a religious. Christmas night will go by there without a Mass, without a single mouth or heart saying the name of Jesus.

They are quite right who say: Pray for France, for she is losing herself. But unhappy as the disorders of France may be, what are they beside the night, the mourning which is Morocco? My thoughts are there night and day, and I am praying. My prayers go there from the foot of the tabernacle and at holy Mass—but not there only. I am not forgetful of everyone else, but I pray for it especially, before anywhere else, more and more. The thought of it never leaves me. But I am completely in the dark as to what could be done to make the star of the Magi shine in that night. Pray and sanctify myself—for the moment that is all I can see, and to accept the cross joyfully, more perfectly, than I have done. To carry it to others one must first accept it joyfully oneself, and I have not yet begun. Prayers, sanctification and suffering—that is where the start must be made, if later Jesus is going to be able to do anything with me.

I am still alone. If I am going to have brothers, I must improve myself, be converted, die like the grain of wheat which if it does not die remains alone.

So pray for my conversion, beloved father, pray that I may at last become faithful to the graces of Jesus. And pray too for Morocco, visible from here across the plains, so close to us yet so far from Jesus. Pray that there may be fulfilled in it that prophecy of Isaias in the breviary lessons for today: *Delebitur foedus vestrum cum morte, et pactum vestrum cum inferno non stabit.*[5]

You know your child venerates and loves you with his whole

[5] Is. 28:18: "Your league with death shall be abolished, and your covenant with hell shall not stand."

heart. Look carefully about you at the midnight Mass, throughout the Christmas season and on New Year's Day, for all the best that is in his heart will be with you then. Be good enough to bless me. I kneel before you with filial respect and devotion in the Heart of the Beloved Jesus.

Brother Charles of Jesus [6]

In the same month he made his annual retreat and during it wrote the following resolutions in his notebook:

1. *Preliminary.* We must imitate Jesus by doing our life's work for the salvation of men in such a way that the word "Jesus," Saviour, is the perfect expression of what we are, just as it signifies perfectly what he is. To do so, we must "be all things to all men, having only one desire in our hearts, to give Jesus to souls."

"As long as you did it to one of these my least brethren, you did it to me. . . . So let your good works shine before men that they may glorify your Father who is in heaven."

We must have a passionate desire to save souls, doing and arranging everything to that end, putting the good of souls before everything, sparing no effort to make perfect use of the seven great means of converting and saving unbelievers Jesus has given us: offerings of the Holy Sacrifice, putting ourselves in the presence of the tabernacle of the Blessed Sacrament, goodness, prayer, penance, good example and personal holiness. "As the pastor is, so are the sheep"—"The good a soul does is directly related to its interior spirit." The sanctification of the peoples of this area is thus in my hands: they will be saved if I become a saint.

"If any man will come after me, let him deny himself and take up his cross and follow me." We must go in by the narrow way,

* Cf. C, pp. 203–6.

seeking the cross so as to follow our crucified Spouse and share his cross and thorns: we must seek for crosses and sacrifices, delighting in them as worldlings do in their pleasures. "If we do not accept our cross, we are not worthy of Jesus."

"Seek . . . the kingdom of God and his justice; and all these things shall be added unto you."—"Be not solicitous for your life, what you shall eat, nor for your body, what you shall put on." We ought to rejoice greatly every time we lack anything.

I should usually divide my time of mental prayer into two parts: during one of them (at least equal to the other) I should contemplate and if necessary meditate; during the other, I should pray for people, for every human being without exception, as well as for those who are in a special sense in my charge. I should say the divine office with extreme care: it is the daily bouquet of fresh roses, the symbol of a love forever young, offered every day to the Beloved, the Spouse.

I ought very, very frequently to make a *spiritual communion.* The only standard by which I measure it should be that of my love, calling a hundred, a thousand times every day on the beloved Saviour of my soul.

"He that heareth you, heareth me"—"Whosoever therefore shall humble himself as this little child, he is the greater in the kingdom of heaven." When in doubt, incline always towards obedience. As often as possible, make acts of obedience, not only so as to be certain of doing the will of God, but also so as to imitate Jesus' submission at Nazareth, to obey Jesus when he asked us to be as small children, and to love Jesus as much as possible in heaven, eternally, taking there that better place set aside for those who have made themselves the least of all by obedience to other men, and the humility such obedience demands.

I am in the house at Nazareth with Mary and Joseph, like a younger brother sitting opposite my elder brother Jesus, who is here night and day in the Sacred Host. I must behave towards my neighbor in a way fitting to this place, this company, as I have seen Jesus do, setting me an example. In the "Fraternity" [7] I must always be humble, gentle and ready to serve as were Jesus, Mary and Joseph at the holy house at Nazareth. To serve others, I need gentleness, humility, abjection and charity.

I must wash the linen of the poor (especially on Maundy Thursday) and regularly clean their rooms, doing as much as possible *myself*. As far as possible, I myself and no one else must do the lowest work of the house, keeping the parts occupied by the native population clean, taking every *service* on myself, to be like Jesus who lived among his apostles as "one who serves." We must be very gentle towards the poor and everyone else, for this too is humility. When I can do so, I must cook for the poor, and carry food and drink to them, not leaving that service to others.

In every sick person I should see, not a human being, but Jesus, and so should show him respect, love, compassion, joy and gratitude at being able to serve him, zeal and gentleness. I should serve the sick as I do the poor, making myself do the lowliest services for them all, as Jesus washed the apostles' feet.

I must tolerate the presence of evil people, as long as their wickedness is not corrupting others—as Jesus tolerated Judas. Resist not evil. I must accede to requests, even unjust ones, out of obedience towards God and so as to do good to souls by humbling myself in this way, treating others as God did. I must continue to do good for the ungrateful, in imitation of God who makes rain fall on the just and unjust alike. "If you show goodness only towards the good, what merit is there?" "Show goodness towards the wicked and ungrateful and hostile, as did God himself." Every living human being, however wicked, is a child of

[7] This was what he called his hermitage at Beni-Abbès, where he welcomed visits by nomads and the people of the village. He liked calling himself the "universal brother."

God, an image of God and a member of Christ's body: there must therefore be respect, love, attention and solicitude for their physical relief, and an extreme zeal for the spiritual perfection of every one of them.

We should not seek for great possessions in order to be able to give large sums in alms: that would be quite contrary to our Lord's example. Like him I should live by the labor of my hands and give a little as he did to those who ask—or have need.

"I am come to call not the just, but sinners." There should be only one desire in my heart, to give Jesus to all men. I should be especially concerned for the lost sheep, the sinners, not leaving the ninety-nine lost sheep in order to stay quietly in the fold with the faithful one. I must overcome the natural severity I feel towards sinners, together with my disgust, and replace them with compassion, interest, zeal and lively care for their souls.

I must want to suffer cold, heat or anything else, liking it, enjoying it, so as to have a bigger sacrifice to offer to God and be more closely united with Jesus. I shall thus be able to glorify him better by offering him a superabundant tribute of sufferings and receive both on earth and in heaven a deeper knowledge and love of Jesus. The less of everything we have, the more like the crucified Jesus we are—the more devoted to the cross we are, the greater glory we give Jesus who is nailed there. Every cross is profitable, for every cross makes us one with Jesus.

I should have nothing more or better than Jesus of Nazareth had it. I should rejoice and long to have less rather than more.

. . . At every moment, *I should live today as though faced with the prospect of dying this evening as a martyr.*

"One thing is necessary": to do at all times what would be most pleasing to Jesus, to be continually ready for martyrdom and accept it *without a shadow of a defence,* as did the divine Lamb, doing so in Jesus, through Jesus and for Jesus.

. . . I should rejoice not in what I have but in what I lack, in lack of success and in penury, for then I have the cross and poverty of Jesus, the most precious possessions the earth can give.

Abjection: service to others. I must decide on a definite number of very lowly daily tasks and do them, as Jesus came to Nazareth "to serve." I must stop that orderly.[8] "Serve, not be served." [9]

On Ash Wednesday, February 25, 1903, Brother Charles of Jesus noted in his journal:

I promise to use *every moment* of my life in saving those members of our Lord who are being lost, doing so by prayer, penance, example, sanctifying myself, by goodness, offering the Holy Sacrifice, the Blessed Sacrament, and the foundation and development of the Little Brothers and Sisters of the Sacred Heart of Jesus, the conversion of Morocco and such other countries as the Sacred Heart may indicate.[10]

At the beginning of this same year, 1903, Brother Charles drew up his great plan for Moroccan missions. Before his conversion he had explored the country for his own enjoyment and now he had a strong longing to return to win souls for God and establish the realm of Christ's love there.

. . . What I think it might be best to do for the conversion of Morocco is organize a little legion of religious, dedicated both to contemplation and good works, living in great poverty by manual labor. Its simple rule might be summed up in three phrases: perpetual adoration of the Blessed Sacrament exposed, imitation of

---

[8] One of the soldiers of the Beni-Abbès garrison had been going out of kindness to the hermitage to do some heavy work there.

[9] Cf. ES, pp. 208–13.

[10] Cf. IS, p. 290.

the hidden life of Jesus at Nazareth, and life in mission countries. Such a little legion would be a vanguard ready to throw itself into the field of Morocco and dig there, at the feet of the Sacred Victim and in the Name of the Sacred Heart of Jesus, a first trench into which the preaching missionaries would then throw themselves as soon as possible afterwards. With this purpose in mind, and with the encouragement of my holy and beloved bishop, Mgr. Bonnet, Bishop of Viviers, I asked and obtained permission from the Right Reverend Apostolic Prefect of the French Sahara to establish myself at a point in his prefecture close to the Moroccan frontier.

Beni-Abbès, a small Saharan oasis on the Moroccan frontier, appeared to be the most suitable place from which to enter Morocco. The neighboring peoples seem to be less hostile than others.

Last Christmas, I felt so urgent a need to take a step forward that I believed I was obeying the Sacred Heart in calling on the souls whose co-operation I can hope for in this matter to start the war against Satan with a crusade of prayers. So far as is possible, I have humbly offered Morocco to the Sacred Heart. I have prayed to Blessed Margaret Mary, asking her to obtain for me the grace of celebrating the Holy Sacrifice there soon.

Since my arrival here, I have been building up relationships with the native inhabitants and especially with the Moroccans. Every day many natives visit the Fraternity of the Sacred Heart, and among them there are Moroccans. In the near future I hope to be able to go with some Moroccans into their country. I should like to go there first for a few days, then for a few weeks, then for some months, and to buy a small property there where a new Fraternity of the Sacred Heart could grow up.

It would thus be possible to advance step by step. Alms and hospitality, the redemption and liberation of slaves, and still more the offering of the Divine Victim will conciliate their hearts and open paths for direct preaching. The more fervent and numerous this silent advance-guard is, the sooner the hour for open preaching will come.

I am alone, and that makes things a little difficult with regard to the small penetration of Morocco I hope to make in a few weeks' time. It would be very useful to have a chosen companion to support me in my weakness, to prevent any possibility of my making a false move, and any possibility of profanation. This ought to be a temptation to many souls, for what I am offering them is the next thing to glory, for the dangers are great. . . .[11]

Every day the Blessed Sacrament was exposed for eight hours. Brother Charles of Jesus was expecting Mgr. Guérin to visit him at the beginning of May. He had not been able to make his confession for six months.

On February 27, he wrote to him:

I am infinitely worthless, yet search as I will I can find no desire in me except *adveniat regnum tuum! sanctificetur nomen tuum!* You ask me if I am ready to go anywhere else besides Beni-Abbès to spread the holy Gospel. To do that I am ready to go to the end of the world and to live till the last judgement.

Do not think that the hope of enjoying the vision of the Beloved more quickly plays any part in my way of life—I want only one thing: to do what is most pleasing to him. If I love fasting and watching, it is because Jesus loved them so much. I am envious of his nights of prayer on the mountain tops, I should like to keep him company. Night is the time for intimate converse, for loving and intimate conversations, the time of the watch kept over the Heart of the Beloved. Alas, I am so cold that I dare not say I am

[11] From his Journal (cf. ES, p. 249 ff.).

in love, but I should like to be in love. I should like those long exchanges by night—that is why I like to keep watch.

I want to say again that although my conscience is not torturing me, far from it—I am too cowardly—I am going to improve my *pulmentum* [12] in filial obedience to you. You may be sure that I am ready to do anything whatsoever for Jesus.

Now I should like to ask something of you myself: pray that I may love; pray that I may love Jesus; pray that I may love his cross; pray that I may love the cross, not for its own sake, but as the only means, the only way of giving glory to Jesus: "The grain of wheat does not bring forth fruit unless it dies . . . And I, if I be lifted up . . . will draw all things to myself." As St. John of the Cross points out, it was at the moment of his supreme abasement, the hour of his death, that Jesus did the most good, that he saved the world. So then ask Jesus that I may truly love the cross, for it is indispensable if we are going to do good to souls. And I carry it very little, I am cowardly. Virtues are ascribed to me which I do not possess—and I am the most fortunate of men. So pray for my conversion, that I may love Jesus and do at all times what would be most pleasing to him. Amen.[13]

On March 9, he wrote to the same prelate again:

What does the Heart of Jesus want? I am the slave of his divine Heart. It is a bondage I do not want to abolish, the fetters of which I pray the divine Beloved to rivet tight for ever and ever. Tell me the will of the Heart of Jesus and I shall do it.[14]

Brother Charles had not lost touch with the Clarist nuns at

[12] Diet.
[13] Cf. ES, pp. 229 ff.
[14] Cf. ES, p. 230.

Nazareth. On May 13, 1903, he wrote to one of them, Sister St. John of the Sacred Heart:

The simplest and best means of uniting ourselves with the Heart of our Spouse is to do, think and say everything with him and as he did, holding ourselves in his presence and imitating him. Whatever we do, say or think, we should tell ourselves: Jesus can see me; during his life on earth he was watching me at this moment; what did he do, think or say in similar circumstances? What would he do, say or think in my position now? *Watch and imitate* him. Jesus himself suggested this very simple method of achieving union with him and perfection to his apostles. The very first words he said to them on the banks of Jordan, when Andrew and John came to him were: *"Come and see."* "Come"—that is, follow me, come with me, follow in my footsteps; imitate me, doing as I do; and "see," that is, watch me, stay with me, contemplate me.

All perfection is to be found in the presence of God and Jesus and in the imitation of Jesus. It is perfectly obvious that anyone doing as Jesus did is perfect. So then we must throw ourselves wholeheartedly into *imitating* him (a task sweeter than honey to the loving heart, and an urgent need for the loving soul, a need that becomes the more compelling as love becomes more ardent) and *watching* him, the divine Spouse (a task no less sweet or indispensable to love). Anyone who loves, loses and buries himself in contemplation of the Beloved.[15]

Nothing came from the journey to Morocco. But in May, Charles de Foucauld was visited by an old friend who was shortly afterwards to be appointed commandant of the oasis district of the Sahara, with supervision of the Hoggar district on the southern

[15] Cf. FMS, p. 43.

edge of the Sahara. Major Laperrine had told Brother Charles about the endless expanse of the Sahara and about the Tuareg tribes. In a letter written in June he urged him to come to the Tuareg.

On December 13, 1903, Brother Charles wrote to the Abbé Huvelin:

Beloved father:

A Holy Christmas and a Holy New Year: May the Heart of Jesus heap graces upon you! I do not need to tell you that the thoughts, heart and prayers of your child are with you. You know that in spite of my worthlessness I love you with all my heart.

I am just ending my annual retreat. Its final resolution is: "I will follow accurately the rule of life I have drawn up for myself." The three main things for which I have to ask Jesus' forgiveness in 1903 are: sensuality, lack of charity towards my neighbor, and lukewarmness towards God.

I have a daily problem about which I want to ask you the will and mind of Jesus. The problem is that of alms. To "give to him that asks" would be to do more harm than good with a people so slothful, brazen and given to begging, as you yourself have told me, and as I see every day. But on the other hand, I am very much afraid that from time to time when turning away impostors I also send away some who are really poor. And I am also afraid of not giving enough. One would have to know everybody, and I cannot do that.

I am also very undecided in the matter of a journey I had planned to make to the south, to the oases of Tuat and Tidikilt, which are quite without a priest, where our soldiers never have the Mass, and the Moslems never see a minister of Jesus. You will recall that having received Mgr. Guérin's three authorizations from you, I was just setting off in September when I was called to Taghit to attend the wounded. But now that peace seems to have been restored, ought I not to go on with my plan? A big question-mark hangs over it as far as I am concerned. I know without asking that Mgr. Guérin would leave it to me: that is why I am asking your advice. If Mgr. Guérin were able and willing to send another priest there, I certainly should not go. My duty would quite clearly be to stay at Beni-Abbès.

But I do not think he will want to send anyone there; indeed, I believe it is *not possible* [16] for him to send anyone. But on the other hand, thanks to personal friendships, I can go there, and I am probably the only priest who *could* at this time and for some time to come—at least unless many unhappy things are changed.

In these circumstances, is it not my duty to go there and establish a forward base—if I may so express it—in the extreme south? I can go and spend two, three or four months there every year, using my journey to advantage by administering or at least offering the sacraments in the garrisons, and letting Moslems see the cross and the Sacred Heart,[17] and telling them a little about our holy religion?

Ought I not to do this?

At the moment it could not be easier for me. They have invited me there and are expecting me.

My nature rebels violently against it. I am ashamed to have to say that I shiver at the thought of going: of leaving empty the tabernacle at Beni-Abbès; of going away to a place where there might (though it is very unlikely) be fighting,[18] and spending myself in journeys that are of no value to the soul. Do not I give greater glory to God by adoring him in solitude? Are not solitude and the life of Nazareth my vocation?

[16] "Ways of spreading religion . . ." Brother Charles noted in his diary under date of July 22 (cf. B, p. 270).

[17] Brother Charles wore a heart and a cross of red cloth sewn to his robe.

[18] And also wounded men, needing the assistance of a priest (see above).

But after reason has said all that, I see those vast areas without a priest, I see myself as the only priest who *can* go there, and I feel myself under extreme and ever growing pressure to go—to go there at least once and base a decision on whether to go again or not on the results and what experience reveals.

Despite reason's arguments against it, and nature's real horror of being away from here, I feel myself under extreme and ever-growing pressure from within to make this journey.

A convoy is leaving for the south on January 10. Should I join it? At the moment I can do so easily and they are expecting me. Should I wait for another? There may not be one for several months, and I have reasons to fear that I shall not then have the same facilities as I have now.

Ought I not to go away at all?

My feelings and conviction are very clear: I ought to go on January 10.[19]

In December, Brother Charles wrote during his retreat:

If I have Jesus, I am bound to him alone: to his words, his example and his will. To possess him, obey him, imitate him, be one with him, lose myself in him by losing my own will in his— all this cries out to me to be completely detached from everything that is not him. The desire to possess nothing but him cries out: detachment! His words cry: detachment! His example cries: detachment! His will cries: detachment!

Continually to see Jesus in myself, making his dwelling with his Father in me . . .

I must work with all my strength to sanctify myself: *mortification, mortification, penance and death!* It is when one suffers most that one most sanctifies oneself and others. "Unless the grain of wheat . . . die, it brings forth nothing . . . If I be lifted up from the earth, I shall draw all things to myself." Jesus is not saving the world by his divine words, miracles or blessings, but by his cross. The most fruitful hour of his life was that of his greatest abasement and prostration, when he was plunged deepest into suffering and humiliation.

Obedience is the measure of love: be perfectly obedient in order to have perfect love.

I must sanctify myself as much as possible, so that I may do all that is possible to me for the glory of God in bringing tabernacles and priests to distant lands where no one knows Jesus, and the greatest feasts, Christmas and Easter, and indeed the whole year go by without a Mass, or a prayer, or a single mouth saying Jesus' name. Then numerous Masses will be said in them and fervent prayers ascend to heaven, and the Christian life will pour out its blessings over them; the Blessed Sacrament will be exposed perpetually day and night on many altars and will be adored by fervent monks and nuns.

The best used hour in our lives is that in which we love Jesus most.

A soul does good, not in proportion to its knowledge or intellect, but to its holiness.

I must embrace all men for God's sake in the same love and the same self-forgetfulness. I must be no more anxious about my own health and life than a tree is about a falling leaf.

We must remember only Jesus, think only of Jesus, counting any loss as a profit insofar as it makes more room in us for thought about and knowledge of Jesus, beside whom everything else is nothing.

"I must keep all my powers for God." [20]

[20] Cf. ES, p. 215 ff.

On January 13, 1904, Brother Charles left Beni Abbès. The important stages on his journey took him to: Adrar, the capital of Tuat (February 2); In-Salah (February 16); In-Zig (April 1). He stayed for some time in the region of In-Salah in order to make a more intensive study of the Tuareg language than was possible while traveling. On February 27, he wrote to Henry de Castries:

My life goes on in an unparalleled calm. It is so pleasant to feel one is in the hands of God, carried by the Creator, supreme Goodness and Love—*Deus caritas est*—the love and the lover, the Spouse of our souls in time and in eternity. It is so pleasant to feel oneself being carried by his hand through this short life towards that eternity of light and love for which he created us.[21]

On May 28, he reached Tit, the central point in the Hoggar district:

Talking, distributing medicines and alms, offering the hospitality of the camp, demonstrating that we are brothers and repeatedly saying that we are all brothers in God and hope one day all to be in the same heaven, praying for the Tuareg with all my heart: this is my life now. . . . My normal vocation is to solitude, stability and silence. But if, extraordinarily, I feel called sometimes to do something else, I can only say: *Ecce ancilla domini.*[22]

On July 15 he wrote to the Abbé Huvelin:

Warmest greetings on your feast-day, beloved father. My wish

[21] Cf. LHC, p. 149.
[22] To Henry de Castries, June 17, 1904 (cf. LCH, p. 154).

for you—my continual prayer for you—is that the will of Jesus may be accomplished in you on earth as it is in heaven.

God has given me the grace of being four months in a country which until now has been closed to the sacred Victim and the holy Gospel. I am doing what I can here: very prudently and discreetly I am trying to give the native people, the Tuareg, confidence in me and persuade them to let friendship rule between us. I am sowing; others will reap.

I am able to celebrate the Holy Sacrifice every day; the sacred Victim is taking possession of his kingdom. I am translating the four Gospels into the Tuareg language. I am trying with all my strength to demonstrate and prove to these poor lost brothers that our religion is nothing but charity and fraternity, and that its badge is a HEART.

I am living from day to day. I shall stay here so long as I can be of use in this country, unless others come to replace me—for there must be someone here.

I am making it my rule to do things I believe will be of great value to souls, but which circumstances will not permit others to do. Thus I think I shall stay in this country so long as I am tolerated here or until I am replaced, and as long as I can work usefully for Jesus' kingdom. At the moment I am a nomad living in a tent, constantly moving from place to place. This is very good for a start, for it permits me to see a great many people and much of the country. But as soon as I can establish myself in fixed quarters and a definite place I shall do so, for I believe that to be my vocation, and that journeys should play only an accidental part in my life. I shall then lead the life of Nazareth in a corner of the Tuareg country, as long as I am tolerated there and would not be more useful elsewhere. But I am not useful anywhere. I shall stay as long as I believe it to be the will of Jesus and while they tolerate me.

Beloved father, no one will realize better than you the importance of the good to be done here; and no one knows better than you the uselessness of your poor child, who is so cowardly, weak, lazy, egotistical, vain, sensual, so spiritually limited, lukewarm and faithless. I beseech you to pray for me. And I ask you, too, to pray for the peoples of the Sahara and Morocco, and especially for the Tuareg. Finally, ask God to send saints and many workers into this part of his field and—if he will—to send me companions.

Once again, I wish you a happy and holy feastday, kneeling before you and beseeching you to bless your unworthy child, who loves and venerates you, and is wholeheartedly devoted to you in the Sacred Heart of Jesus.

Brother Charles of Jesus [23]

Brother Charles' longing for brothers and sisters to share his life was growing continually. On December 15, 1904, he wrote to a dedicated woman whose life was one of great sufferings:

Dear sister in Jesus:

Being in great need of prayers, I am coming to look for them and ask for them in my family—the close-knit family of the Heart of Jesus. Since receiving the last letter from the Abbé Veyras, dated Good Friday, I have written to him several times without receiving a reply. Perhaps he is sick. Or has he changed his address? Besides him, your are the only member of our family whose address I know. Therefore, feeling the need and duty of bringing together all the forces I can find for Jesus' work, I am writing to you.

In turning to you, I want to ask you not only to give me your

[23] Cf. C, pp. 221 ff.

own help, but to bring together every power available to you for this work for Jesus, which it is so clear to me must be undertaken, and at which I believe so firmly I ought to work. So please show this letter to our father, the Abbé Crozier, and ask the help, prayers and sacrifices of those of our brothers and sisters whose names Jesus will reveal to you for this work for Jesus at which I am laboring.

The work to which I have long seen I ought to dedicate my life is the building up of two little families, one called the "Little Brothers of the Sacred Heart of Jesus," and the other the "Little Sisters of the Sacred Heart of Jesus," both with the same aim: the glorification of God by the imitation of the hidden life of Jesus, the perpetual adoration of the sacred Host and the conversion of unbelievers. They would both take the same form: they would be small, enclosed fraternities with about twenty brothers or sisters, in which, following the Rule of St. Augustine and special constitutions (with solemn vows when Holy Church permits), the hidden life of Jesus of Nazareth will be followed as faithfully as possible, and the most Blessed Sacrament, exposed day and night, will be perpetually adored in love, adoration, sacrifice, prayer, manual labor, poverty, abasement, recollection and silence. They will be in the most out-of-the-way parts of non-Christian countries, so that Jesus will be brought to the places where he is least known, and search may be made with him for his most lost and abandoned sheep.

Not knowing any more lost, abandoned, deserted country, none more lacking in workers for the Gospel than the Sahara and Morocco, I have asked and obtained permission to set up a tabernacle on their frontiers, and bring a few brothers together there in adoration of the sacred Victim. I have been living here for several years up till now, alone—*mea culpa, mea culpa, mea culpa.* Unless the grain of wheat falling to the ground dies, it remains alone; if it dies, it brings forth much fruit. I have not died, so I am alone. Pray for my conversion that, dying, I may bear fruit. . . .

I am staying here with the good and holy Apostolic Prefect of the Sahara by whose authority I do this work in his prefecture. In a few days' time I shall return to my cell beside the lonely tabernacle, feeling more deeply than ever that Jesus wants me to work to found this double family. How shall I work for it? By praying, sacrificing myself, dying, sanctifying myself: in short, by loving him.

Although I am a sinner and unworthy to belong to this inner family circle [24], I am coming to you to ask and beseech you to help me. "Our Lord is in need." His hidden life at Nazareth, with its great poverty, abasement and recollection, is not being imitated. The adoration of the Sacred Heart should be the foundation of the life of every human being. . . .

The Sahara, which is eight or ten times as big as France and more densely populated than is generally believed, has thirteen priests. In the interior of Morocco, which is as large as France and has eight or ten million inhabitants, there is not a single priest, tabernacle or altar.

"Our Lord is in need." The days—given us to love him, imitate him, save souls with him—are flowing by, and people are not loving him, imitating him, or saving souls with him.

May our Beloved, our brother Jesus, inspire and guide you. may he teach you how to help me in accordance with his will.

It was at this time of the year, during the hard winter season, that the most holy Virgin, carrying within her the Infant Jesus,

[24] Cf. the beginning of this letter. The "family" was a group of priests and laypeople who had dedicated their lives to the Sacred Heart of Jesus. This was the first adumbration of the "Union of Brothers and Sisters of the Sacred Heart" which Brother Charles was to call into being in the year 1909, and which was to grow until it became the numerous and multiform spiritual family we know today.

was traveling with St. Joseph from Nazareth to Bethlehem over the difficult roads to Israel. A few days afterwards, our Lord was born in a humble cave. How great were their obscurity, their sufferings, their outward and apparent poverty! What depths of blessedness, glory and light there were within, in the souls of Mary and Joseph, and especially of Jesus. In trying at this holy season to make myself one with our brother Jesus and our parents Mary and Joseph, I am also making myself wholeheartedly one with all our brothers and sisters. I shall be there with them more fully than ever at Christmas, joining them before the manger. And every day I shall pray especially for you, my sister in Jesus: it is the will of the Beloved, for he has brought me especially close to you.

If you write to me, do not fail to give me your advice. Tell me everything you think might serve to give glory to Jesus. Talk to me as one would talk in the cave at Bethlehem and under that roof at Nazareth.

May Jesus be with you and live in you.

Your humble brother in Jesus

Brother Charles of Jesus

Most Sacred Heart of Jesus, thy kingdom come! [25]

It had become impossible for Brother Charles to stay in Hoggar any longer. After staying with Mgr. Guérin at Ghardaia, at the end of 1901 he went back to Beni-Abbès to throw himself into the work of founding his communities. He wrote from there to the Abbé Huvelin on Tuesday in Holy Week, April 18, 1905.

My beloved father:

Your child is coming to join his alleluias with your own. I am sending you this short note to tell you that I shall surely be with

[25] Extracts from a letter to Susanne Perret, dated from Ghardaia on December 15, 1904 (cf. TPF, p. 175 ff.).

you during this Holy Week and through Easter Week, rejoicing with you here below in the infinite and unalterable bliss of the Beloved, expecting that by his great mercy I shall hereafter rejoice with you in heaven, if I do not prove myself unworthy.

Recently I have been laboring under a difficulty, which now looks to me as though it was pure temptation. I have been urgently invited to spend the summer among the Tuareg, and I have been worried. It is a vast country without a priest and at the moment closed to all priests. And when they do invite a priest, almost demanding that he go there, he refuses. That seems blameworthy to me—the more so because he seems to be refusing suffering, for such long journeys are not made without fatigue.

On the other hand, although the country is closed to priests at the present time, it is certain that if the Right Reverend Apostolic Prefect *wished*, he could find a way into it within a few months. My refusal involves only a brief delay.

Even from the point of view of the apostolate, I think I should do more for the conversion of souls by staying here, striving to bring together a number of brothers who would become a fitting instrument for doing a great deal of good in a great many places, than by making long, not very rewarding journeys on my own.

Lastly, as has been made clear to me so often, my vocation is to the life of Nazareth, the life of a little brother of the Sacred Heart of Jesus, and I do not think I could better serve him who alone is to be adored than by leading it perfectly myself, following strictly the rule I have drawn up for the others.

I ought from now on to bury myself in the life of Nazareth, as he buried himself in it for thirty years, and as I should want my brothers to bury themselves in it, as far as possible doing the good that he did, without trying to do things he did not try to do. And I should look on everything else, attractive as it might seem, as temptation from him who can change himself into an angel of light. This is the rule I think I should make for the last part of my life—which will not last as long as the thirty years Jesus spent at Nazareth.

If I am wrong, tell me so.

I know, beloved father, that God is testing you at the present time, by binding your hands. A simple "yes" or "no" will give me Jesus' answer: "He that heareth you, heareth me."

Kneeling at your feet, I beseech you to bless your child, who though so unworthy and valueless, loves and venerates you filially with all his heart in the Heart of Jesus.

Brother Charles of Jesus [26]

Having received a cable from Mgr. Guérin asking him to accept Laperrine's suggestion that he should spend the summer at Hoggar, Brother Charles of Jesus set out on May 3, 1905, taking with him his catechumen Paul.

On May 18, he wrote to the Abbé Huvelin from Sali in the district of Tuat:

Beloved Father:

I am on the way, thinking of you, praying for you, united with you in the Heart of Jesus at the beginning of an eternal union in him.

How good you are, and how moved I was by the two hundred francs you sent me! I am trying to make the best possible use of them, using them in Jesus' work according to his will: they will be given in alms to dispose souls to love Jesus and like his servants. I thank you from my heart.

I am almost certainly going to spend June, July, August and September among the Tuareg, returning in October. *I want to ask you what to do about my return.* There are three possibilities: first, to return to Beni-Abbès and stay there; second, to settle

[26] Cf. C, pp. 230 ff.

among the Tuareg and stay there; and third—although it would interfere with my general vocation to the hidden life—to divide my time for several years between Beni-Abbès and the Tuareg, until circumstances make it clear that I can return to silence and the enclosure, either at Beni-Abbès or among the Tuareg. In the light of my present journey, I am inclined towards this last course, especially if matters fall out in such a way that it becomes possible to arrange a permanent residence among the Tuareg.

What I am proposing to Mgr. Guérin is that as soon as I return from In-Salah I should go directly to Beni-Abbès and from there to the motherhouse [27] near Algiers to see him and collect a companion—someone I knew who was also known to him, whom I have asked him to train for me. Then I shall take my companion quickly to the Tuareg, and help him to settle there. For some time I shall divide my time between this new settlement and Beni-Abbès—until you consider such journeys ought no longer to be necessary and I can go back to my life, the hidden life of Nazareth. Afterwards, I should lead the life of Nazareth at Beni-Abbès, or among the Tuareg, or elsewhere, as circumstances dictate—I still have a leaning towards Beni-Abbès.

In the course of my present journey I shall endeavor to prepare and organize my fixed home among the Tuareg, so as to be able to take the companion I have asked Mgr. Guérin to train for me straight there on my return.

I feel very weak, cowardly and incompetent. Pray for me that I may know what Jesus wants.

I kneel at your feet, beloved father, to ask you to bless me. You know that I love and venerate you as a son and with all my heart in the Heart of our beloved Jesus.

Brother Charles of Jesus [28]

[27] This was the Maison Carrée, the motherhouse of the White Fathers, to which order Mgr. Guérin belonged.

[28] Cf. C, pp. 233 ff.

While traveling, Brother Charles kept a diary, a daybook of his journeys and apostolic work. On July 22, 1905, while still on his journey, he made the following notes:

Love, obey, imitate—a life of faith, hope and charity. Love Jesus, obey and imitate him. Obedience will put you into the situation that he wills for you. When his will does not show you clearly that he is willing an alteration in your situation, remain in the *status quo*. But always imitate him. *Without imitation of him, there can be no perfection.* In your own case especially, for imitating him is your vocation, duty and obligation at every moment of your life. Imitation of him has always been your first resolution in all your retreats: *in capite libri* [29]: It stands at the head of your life and gives it its direction. Jesus has put you into the life of Nazareth to stay there for ever: the missionary life and the life of solitude are exceptional for you as they were for him. Practise them whenever his will indicates clearly that you should; but as soon as there is no such clear indication, return to the life of Nazareth.

Long for the foundation of the Little Brothers and Little Sisters of the Sacred Heart of Jesus. Follow their rule as one follows a general directive, without making it a binding obligation. Until it really becomes possible to lead the life of the Little Brothers and Little Sisters in a Nazareth with a monastic enclosure, whether you are alone or in a company of a few brothers, take the life of Nazareth as your aim, for all purposes, in all its simplicity and breadth, using the rule only as a general directive assisting you in certain matters to enter into the life of Nazareth. Thus, for example, until the Little Brothers and Sisters are officially established, you should, like Jesus at Nazareth, have no particular dress, no enclosure, and no dwelling far from all habitation, but

[29] "In the head of the book," cf. Heb. 10:7 and Ps. 39:8 (Vulg.).

should be near to a village—like Jesus at Nazareth; doing not less than eight hours work a day—like Jesus at Nazareth—manual work or otherwise, but manual work as often as possible. Like Jesus at Nazareth, you should have neither big estates nor large houses; neither your expenses nor even your alms should be big, but extreme poverty should show itself everywhere. In a word, in everything, follow Jesus at Nazareth. Use the Little Brothers' rule to help you lead this life like another book of piety. Always withdraw resolutely from anything which would not represent perfect imitation of this life.

Do not seek to organize and prepare the ground for the foundation of the Little Brothers of the Sacred Heart of Jesus. Being alone, live as though you were always going to be alone. If there are two or three or more of you, live as though there were never going to be any more. Pray like Jesus, as much as Jesus, like him always giving a very important place to prayer. Like him again, give an important place to manual labor—which is not time taken from prayer, but given to it: time given to manual labor is a time of prayer. The life of Nazareth can be led everywhere. Lead it where it will be of most service to your neighbor.[30]

He reached Tamanrasset at the heart of the Hoggar among the Tuareg. He had wanted to reach as far as this in his ceaseless southward pursuit of the most abandoned of the sheep. On December 1, 1905, he wrote to the Abbé Huvelin:

Beloved father:

I have just made my annual retreat and have been asking God what I ought to do in 1906.

It seems to me that, in total forgetfulness of myself, I ought to

[30] Cf. OS, pp. 368 ff.

do whatever I can do best for the salvation of the unbelieving peoples of these lands. By what means? By the presence of the most Blessed Sacrament, the offering of the Holy Sacrifice, prayer, penance, good example, goodness, and personal sanctification. By using these means myself and doing what I can to increase the number of those using them among these nations, and of those who, without living among them, use them for their benefit.

Until other priests go to the Beni-Abbès and the Hoggar districts, I must continue to divide my time between them. I could not dream of abandoning either one of them while both districts are otherwise so abandoned. I shall have to share my time a little more equally between them by giving a little more to Hoggar, which is the more remote and wild.

For the moment, it is necessary for me to stay quite a long time yet in Hoggar, so as to demonstrate clearly that I really am settled here and to tie firmly the bonds of my acquaintance with the natives and let them grow used to me.

However, I must not stay so long here before going to Beni-Abbès that I become a stranger there and lose what ground I have gained there.

To make a firm foothold in the Hoggar I ought to stay here until October 1906—to my regret, for that will mean a twenty-month absence from Beni-Abbès, which is a lot. But it seems necessary for the sake of starting at Hoggar. If God does not direct me otherwise, either through the Abbé Huvelin or through the Reverend Father Guérin, or through circumstances, or by some other means, I shall stay at Tamanrasset until October 1906. Then in October I shall leave for Beni-Abbès so as to begin Advent there. I shall stay at Beni-Abbès until Easter 1907, and then leave immediately afterwards, so as to reach Tamanrasset about May 15. Between Christmas and Easter 1907, I shall aim to see the Reverend Father Guérin.

As for going to France to let the chief of the Tuareg spend some time there, it is not possible: it is not even to be thought of.

1906 holds no manual work for me except the work of the sacristy and the care of the sick. All the rest of my working time will have to be used in studying the Tuareg language, and especially in trying to make the study of it easier for those God will send me.

I shall have to write a few letters to priests I know, to try to get one or two companions to work for the good of souls. I shall send the letters to the Abbé Huvelin, who will despatch them or not, as seems good to him.

I must go on putting the Mass before everything and say it while traveling in spite of the rise in expenses that causes. Each Mass is like Christmas, and charity is more important than poverty.

That, briefly, is what I feel I ought to do, beloved father. I am putting it before you and saying as always: speak and I shall obey —"he who heareth you, heareth me."

Pray hard, beloved father, for the Sahara, Morocco and the Tuareg among whom I am living.[31]

On December 15, 1905, he wrote to one of his friends:

It is only by looking out beyond this world, where everything passes away and dies, that we can know the true joy of hope in another life, to which this is only the prelude: a life where the good done here below will have its reward, and where the thirst of our spirits and hearts for light, truth and love will be fully and eternally satisfied.

I am happy, very happy, in this hope and in faith in the truths God has revealed to us—truths beautiful as a poem, as the most

[31] Cf. C, pp. 246 ff.

beautiful of poems, for there are no poems in the world as beautiful as a simple treatise on dogmatic theology, the poem of divine love, on a different plane of wonder and beauty from the bare poems of our earthly loves. In this faith and hope, in the contemplation of this beauty and the fulfillment of the law of charity, the foundation of all Christian morality, "love all human beings as God loves them" my days flow by in a profound peace.[32]

The following passage is an extract from his diary, dated May 17, 1906:

Paul left the Fraternity this morning. O God, make it possible for me to be able to go on celebrating the Holy Sacrifice! Grant that this soul may not be lost. Save it.

During the six festal days between Holy Thursday and Easter Tuesday, I made a kind of retreat. The following is a summary of my resolutions:

1. I must remember to what kind of life it is I have been called: the imitation of Jesus at Nazareth; the adoration of the sacred Host exposed; the silent sanctification of unbelieving peoples by carrying Jesus among them; adoring him and imitating his hidden life.

2. I must remember always to imitate Jesus in his life at Nazareth.

3. I must remember penance, the narrow way, Jesus' cross at Nazareth.

4. I must remember Jesus' poverty at Nazareth.

5. I must remember the lowliness and humble manual labor of Jesus at Nazareth.

6. I must remember the withdrawal, the silence of Jesus at Nazareth.

[32] From a letter to Commandant Lacroix (cf. AS, vol. II, p. 44).

7. I must remember Jesus' distance from the world and the things of the world at Nazareth.

8. I must remember Jesus' life of spiritual communion, adoration, interior prayer, petition and vigils at Nazareth.

9. I must remember to have a zeal for souls, seeking to bring them together around the Sacred Victim in these lands of unbelievers, to build up a small family in imitation of Jesus' life at Nazareth.

10. I must remember to show zeal for souls in charity, goodness and well-doing towards all human beings, like Jesus at Nazareth.

11. I must remember to show zeal for souls by gentleness, humility and forgiveness of injuries, the quiet acceptance of ill-treatment, like Jesus at Nazareth.

12. I must remember to show zeal for souls by giving a good example, like Jesus at Nazareth.

13. I must remember to show zeal for souls by prayer, penance and personal sanctification, like Jesus at Nazareth.

14. I must remember to let the Heart of Jesus live in my heart, so that it may be no longer I who live, but the Heart of Jesus living in me, as it lived at Nazareth.[33]

In 1906, Brother Charles had only one desire, to have someone with him so as to be better able to fulfill his apostolate through the presence of Christ in the Eucharist and the Gospel among those who did not know him.

A novice of the White Fathers, Brother Michael, wanted to follow him. Brother Charles went immediately to the Maison Carrée, the White Fathers' novitiate.

Accompanied by Brother Michael, Brother Charles of Jesus

---

[33] Cf. TPF, p. 191, and OS, pp. 375 ff.

*left the Maison Carrée on December 10. On December 25, he
celebrated Mass at Beni-Abbès, and on December 27, they both
left for Tamanrasset.*

*The year 1907 was very hard. On March 6, Brother Michael
turned back from El-Golea. Brother Charles, having tasted the
great hope of having a companion, was extremely disappointed
and felt more alone than ever. In addition, having made himself
poor so as to carry the Eucharist everywhere, the thought of no
longer having a server at Mass, and thus not being able to celebrate the Holy Sacrifice, was added torment to him. But he
scarcely hesitated. In July 1907 he wired Mgr. Guérin: Try to
obtain permission for celebration Holy Mass alone.*

At the same time he wrote to Mgr. Guérin:

I have often asked myself the question you are posing me:
would it be better to stay at Hoggar without being able to celebrate Mass, or to celebrate it and not go there? Being the only
priest able to go to Hoggar, while there are many who can
celebrate the most Holy Sacrifice, I think it is better in spite of
everything to go to Hoggar, leaving to God the problem of giving
me a way of saying Mass if it is his will (it has always been
possible up till now, by the most varied of means).

Formerly I tended to see on one side the *Infinite,* the holy Sacrifice, and on the other the *finite,* everything apart from God, and
was always ready to sacrifice anything to celebrate Holy Mass.
But there must have been a mistake in my reasoning here, for
from the time of the apostles the greatest saints have in certain
circumstances sacrificed the possibility of celebrating to works of
spiritual charity, in order to make journeys, and so on. If experience shows that I may have to remain at Tamanrasset for a
very long time without being able to celebrate, I think I shall have
to stay there for shorter periods, not hesitating to join company

with military detachments, *which is not at all the same thing as living alone.* It is good to live alone in the land; one can do things there, even though they are of no great importance, for one becomes "at home" there—easily available to others and quite "ordinary." Then, at Tamanrasset, even without daily Mass, there is still the most Blessed Sacrament, regular prayer, long hours of adoration, deep silence and recollection for me, and grace for the whole land radiated by the Sacred Host.

I saw the foundation at In-Salah as a great grace, thinking of you and the future rather than of myself. I shall no doubt pass through it in my comings and goings, though at longer intervals than in the past, and I shall try to establish some kind of relationship with the poor and get them used to trusting the "marabout," [34] but I am a *monk* not a *missionary,* my business is with silence, not words—and to be influential at In-Salah one would have to nurse relationships, paying calls and accepting visits, and that is not my vocation. I am trying only to do a little towards preparing the way for the work which will be yours.[35]

He traveled on alone to Tamanrasset, from where he wrote to the Abbé Huvelin on November 22, 1907:

Beloved father:

I would like this to reach you for Christmas, or at the latest by January 1, but I have little hope that it will. God grant it may reach you at a time pleasing to him! Its purpose is to tell you again what you already know, that unworthy and worthless as he is, your child loves you with all his heart, and thinks of you and prays for you with all his heart. It is a very long time—more than two months—since I received mail from France, and I know

[34] Arabic–a man who leads a holy life, a hermit.
[35] From a letter dated July 2, 1907 (cf. B, pp. 347 ff.).

neither when I shall receive any, nor when this letter can be sent.

Here I should have everything I could want if I had the Holy Mass. I have permission to say it without a server, but not to say it completely alone, in the absence of any other Christian whatsoever. Mgr. Guérin has been kind enough to ask for it for me, but has not been able to get it. The result is I have been able to celebrate only four or five times since July by taking advantage of the transitory visits of a few Frenchmen. But I have the most Blessed Sacrament, and I renew the sacred species when passing Christians make it possible for me to say Mass. The most Blessed Sacrament and solitude are blessings I am coming to appreciate more and more.

According to my earlier plans, I ought to have long since been in In-Salah. But I shall probably be here for at least two and a half months yet. I think Jesus' plan for me is that I should prepare the way for the workers he will send to follow me, and in fulfilling it I have been preparing a short Tuareg grammar and two small lexicons. The grammar and one of the lexicons are ready, and since I have unusual opportunities for working at the moment—one of the Tuareg is helping me a great deal—I think I ought to make good use of this chance to finish the other lexicon. So I shall stay here until it is finished. I am planning to leave here after the Purification, traveling with the Holy Family as it flees into Egypt, visiting Mgr. Guérin in March and spending a few days with him, and reaching Beni-Abbès at the beginning of April to spend the whole summer there, returning here in the autumn.

There is nothing particular to be said about my soul. I am working a great deal—I am having to do so to make the best use of my valuable assistant; his time is limited and I am paying him dearly. I thirst for and need to give a longer time to prayer and reading—I thirst, too, for the Sacraments and the Mass. They will come at the right time, when it is pleasing to Jesus. I believe I am doing his will. My presence here seems to do very little good, but my belief is that the presence of the Divine Master in the tabernacle is in fact doing a great deal of good.

I should like to ask your advice on one point. Next to nothing is being done for the native peoples of our Algeria; for the most part our civilians are seeking only to enlarge the wants of the natives, so as to make bigger profits from them. The military administer them by letting them go their own way, without seriously trying to help them to make progress; some develop a taste for the Arab way of life and become half-Arab themselves. The clergy concern themselves no more with the natives than as if they did not exist—with the exception of the White Fathers. Even the White Fathers, whose order was founded for the sakes of these natives, finding the work very unrewarding have turned their attention to the Negroes of Equatorial Africa. They are making all their efforts there and not now in Algeria, where there is an insignificant number of missionaries whose effect is nil.

The result is that after we have had control of more than three millions of Moslems here for more than seventy years, their moral advance amounts almost to nothing at all, while the million Europeans living in Algeria lead a quite separate life, without in any way entering into the life of the country. They know nothing of its peoples' problems, and see them always as foreigners and most of the time as enemies. This is not observing the duties of a nation with colonies—the brotherhood, which no one denies should exist between men, prescribes quite different ones: we should be thinking of these nations as backward brothers for whose education we are responsible, whose minds and characters it is our duty to raise as high as possible; in short, we ought to do our duty towards them as good brothers.

In the Sudan, in the colonies in Negro territory, it is much worse! I have not seen them, but am close enough here to the Sudan for echoes of what goes on there to reach me. It is clear from the main lines of the stories I hear from those coming from those parts that too many there seek only to serve their own low personal interests, and often do not hesitate over the means. Thus in this vast colonial empire, acquired within the space of a few years, an empire which could be a source of so many blessings for these backward nations, there is nothing but cupidity and violence, without any concern for the peoples' good. Of course, everyone who has read his catechism and knows he ought to love his neighbor knows what a nation's duties are towards its colonies. But alas, so many people take no notice of the catechism, and even those who know it sometimes need a sermon to bring the truth more forcibly before their eyes.

With this evil in mind, and thinking of the duty towards these people that is not now being done—a duty not of a few persons only, but of all without exception who come into contact with them—I have for some months been longing to see a good book, attractive in appearance and easy to read, written by a lay person so it would find a bigger readership, a book that would go into all these things and show clearly what we ought to be doing for our backward brothers. It should be written, not in the dry style and form of a treatise, but in a moving way that would touch the hearts of men of good will. It should show not only the path to be followed but also give encouragement to take it by moving those who can be moved.

Cut off from everyone as I am, I cannot meet anyone whom I might ask to write such a book. It ought to be written by a layman. Can you think of anyone? There is one name in my mind: René Bazin, who wrote *Les Oberlé*. Can you think of anyone? Advise me—or better, take action yourself—for you know, you are in Paris, you know everyone and can do something. There is a great work of charity to be done in this—one responding to an extreme need. Of course, no book will change the fact of things, but it could have an effect on souls of good will, awakening, enlightening, warming them, bringing them to the point of action.[36]

Tamanrasset, Christmas 1907

Beloved father:

A good and holy Christmas! From my whole heart my poor prayers are with you today, asking the Beloved to bring his work in you to perfection, to live more and more fully in you, to glorify his name in and through you, to reign in and through you, and to fulfill his will in and through you as it is fulfilled in heaven. May the Infant Jesus bless you from his manger, in the expectation of the eternal reunion. I am going to write no more than this short note today, I want you to have your child's Christmas greetings and to tell you how completely he is still with you, worthless as he is.[37]

It had not rained for seventeen months, and there was famine in the Hoggar. Brother Charles fell gravely ill, and his sickness was made worse by the fact that as an act of charity he had shared out his stores among the children.

January 1, 1908

Beloved father:

From afar, I am making the New Year's Day visit I owe you as your son, bringing you my good wishes at early dawn: a good

[36] Cf. C, pp. 273–7.
[37] Cf. C, p. 278.

and holy New Year—and heaven too! May Jesus bless you, and live ever more fully in you, and through you in others. May he lead you to be and do whatever is most pleasing to him at all times, and after the trials of earth, may he give you heaven.

I want to renew the request I made in an earlier letter asking you about a much needed book hitting the right note—and making it heard—concerning our duties towards the millions of people inhabiting the suddenly much enlarged French colonial empire.

I once again ask you to take those steps you can take so much better than I, being what I am not, knowing what I do not know, and being acquainted with those I do not know. If you do not think you ought to take them, guide and advise me: tell me whom to contact, and powerless as I am, I will do it. If you think I ought not to do it either, as your obedient child I will not do so. But believe what has been told you by this child of yours, who has now become almost an old man and is living in the midst of infinite miseries that no one is doing anything about, or wants to do anything about. Those here could and should do so much good—on the contrary, they aggravate the lamentable moral and intellectual condition of these races, seeing in them only an opportunity for material profit. What we Christians, professing a religion of love, are showing these people, and what unbelieving Frenchmen, proclaiming fraternity from the rooftops, are showing them, is neglect, or ambition, or avarice—and in almost every case, indifference, aversion and harshness.

And now I am leaving you for today, beloved father, asking our beloved Jesus once more to give you a good and holy New Year, every grace and benediction, and heaven too.

May Jesus bless you this Christmas! May he bless you in the New Year! For you, I ask from him neither health nor any other earthly thing, but that he may fulfill the will of his Heart in you: for he knows better than we do what is best for you, and no one longs as much as he does to give it you. May his name be hallowed in you! May his kingdom come in and through you! May his will be done in and through you as it is in heaven!

There is no need for me to commend myself to your prayers. You know my troubles, and you know how much I need your prayers. More than twenty-one years ago you brought me to Jesus, and you have been my father. It is almost eighteen years since I entered the monastery, and I am in my fiftieth year. What a harvest I ought to bring forth both for myself and others! But instead there is misery and nakedness for myself and not the least good for others. It is by their fruits that trees are known— and this shows me what I am. So pray hard for your poor, most unworthy child.

I am kneeling at your feet and asking you to bless me. You know that I love and venerate you as would a son and with all my heart in the Heart of the beloved Jesus.

Brother Charles of Jesus [38]

Thus Brother Charles chose to be alone at Tamanrasset and even to be deprived of his Mass. At the same time, his health was a great trial to him. But from his difficulties, setbacks and his very sufferings there was born great hope in his heart, and at fifty years of age he produced a scheme of evangelization on the largest scale. On June 1, 1908 he wrote to Mgr. Guérin:

There is a saying in Holy Scripture that I think we should always remember. It says that Jerusalem will be rebuilt *in angustia temporum.*[39] We have to work *in angustia temporum* all our lives. Our difficulties are not a transitory state of affairs, to be allowed

---

[38] Cf. C, p. 279 ff.
[39] "In straightness of times." Dan. 9:25.

to pass by, like a squall of wind, so that we can work on when
the weather grows calm. No, they are the normal state of affairs
and we should reckon on being *in angustia temporum* all our lives
so far as the good we want to do is concerned.[40]

*A few days later, on June 9, he wrote to the Abbé Caron, one
of his friends:*

The corner of the Sahara where I am digging alone extends 1250
miles from north to south, and 625 miles from east to west. There
are 100,000 Moslems in the area, and not a single Christian, apart
from French soldiers of all ranks. And there are not many of
these: eighty or a hundred scattered over the whole expanse, for in
the Saharan squadrons only the officers are French, the soldiers
being natives. In the seven years I have been here I have not made
a single real conversion. Two baptisms—but God knows what the
souls baptized are now and will be in the future. One was a small
child who is being brought up by the White Fathers—and God
knows how he will turn out. The other is a poor, blind old woman;
what goes on in her poor head and how far is her conversion real?
Its value in serious terms is nothing. And I can add something
sadder still: the longer I go on, the more I come to believe that
it is no use at the moment to try to make individual converts (except in special cases), for the level of the mass of the people is
too low, their attachment to the faith of Islam is too strong, and
the intellectual state of the inhabitants makes it very difficult at
the moment for them to recognize the falseness of their religion
and the truth of ours.

Except in exceptional cases anyone seeking to bring about individual conversions today would have that worst of all things:
conversions that are self-interested and assumed. These Moslems,

[40] Cf. ES, p. 238.

who are semi-barbarians, must be approached in a different way from the idolators and fetishists, a completely savage people, barbarians whose religion is wholly inferior. Then again, one needs another approach to the civilized inhabitants. It is possible to set the Catholic faith before the civilized inhabitants directly: they are equipped to understand grounds of credibility and to recognize their truth. One can do the same with the completely barbaric, because their superstitions are so inferior that they are easily made to realize the superiority of the religion of the one God. It seems that with the Moslems the right way would be to civilize them first, to educate them, making them into people like us; when that has been done, their conversion will almost have been accomplished too, for Mohammedanism cannot stand up in the face of education—history and philosophy expose its errors, and its falls like night before day.

Thus the work to be done here, as among all Moslems, is one of moral uplift: raising them morally and intellectually by all possible means, coming close to them, having contact with them, tying the bonds of friendship with them, breaking down their prejudices against us through daily friendly relations, and changing their ideas by the manner and example of our lives. Then we must concern ourselves with this real education—in a word, we must educate them completely. By means of schools and colleges, we must teach them the things taught in schools and colleges, and through daily and close contact with them we must instruct them in the things one learns through one's family—we must become their family.

When this objective has been gained, their ideas will be completely changed, and at the same time their customs will have improved. It will then be easy to bring them to the Gospel. God could, of course, do all this. If it were his will, he could convert the Moslems by his grace in a moment; but up till now it has not been his will. It would even seem that it is not in accordance with his designs to convert them through holiness alone, for if holiness alone were needed, how was it that it was not granted to St. Francis of Assisi to convert them?

All that remains therefore is to make use of what seem to be the most reasonable means, while making oneself as holy as one can and remembering that one does good insofar as one *is* good. The slow and unrewarding means at our disposal for use among a people who reject us, calling us "savages" and "heathen" and who are so far from us in language and customs and so many other ways—our slow and unrewarding means are education through contact and instruction. Above all, we must not be discouraged by difficulties, but must remind ourselves that the more difficult a work is, the slower and more unrewarding it is, the more necessary it is to set to work with great dispatch and make great efforts. We should always keep in mind that saying of St. John of the Cross: "We should not measure our labors by our weakness, but our efforts by our tasks."

But faced with this task, what should one person alone do?

By vocation, I ought to be living a hidden life in solitude, not talking and traveling. On the other hand, some traveling is required of me by the needs of the souls in these lands where I am alone—so long as there are no other workers here. I am trying to reconcile these two things. I have two hermitages a thousand miles apart. Every year I spend three months in the northern one, six months in the southern one and three months coming and going. When I am at one of the hermitages, I live there as an enclosed monk, trying to build for myself a life of work and prayer—the life of Nazareth. On my journeys, I think of the flight into Egypt and the annual journeys of the holy family to Jerusalem. Both at my hermitages and when traveling, I try to make contact as much as possible with the native peoples.[41]

[41] Cf. ES, pp. 255–8.

Brother Charles decided to go to France to try to awaken vocations and found a society of lay people who would live the Gospel in their everyday life and would go to mission countries to do so. He landed at Marseilles on February 17 and left again on March 7. His most important meeting was with Mgr. Bonnet,[42] who had given approval to the statutes of the Union of Brothers and Sisters of the Sacred Heart of Jesus.

On returning to Africa, he wrote to the Abbé Caron on March 11:

I have long been tormented by the thought of the spiritual abandonment of so many unbelievers, and especially by that of the Moslems and unbelievers of our colonies. At the same time I have seen love of material things and vanity taking an ever growing hold on the Christian world. After my last retreat a year ago, I jotted down on paper a scheme for a Catholic association with three aims: to bring Christians back to a life in conformity with the Gospel by drawing to their attention the example of Him who is the only true model; to make love for the holy Eucharist grow among them as our unique possession and our all; and to awaken among them an effective movement towards the conversion of unbelievers, leading them especially to fulfillment of the strict duty binding on all Christians to give a Christian education to the unbelievers in their colonies.

Our work for the conversion of unbelievers ought not to be limited merely to material gifts, but rather ought to lead to the settlement among them of agricultural workers, businessmen, skilled workers, property owners and so on. Good Christians of all kinds would be valuable support for the missionaries, drawing unbelievers to the faith by their example, goodness and friendship,

---

[42] His bishop in the Diocese of Viviers, of which Foucauld was an unattached priest.

and forming solid centers around which former unbelievers could collect as individual conversions take place. The intensity of Christian life that should develop in such a confraternity, and the duty of converting unbelievers held continually in mind, should be also a valuable source of increase in vocations both to the priesthood and to missionary orders of monks and nuns. This confraternity would make lay missionaries, as it were, of good Christians living in the world; it would lead them to leave their native country to become lay missionaries among the most lost sheep, by showing them that the conversion of these is a duty of Catholic nations, and that it is a beautiful and Christian thing to devote one's life to it.

The duties towards unbelievers of those brothers and sisters who are not priests or religious would be all the more important because they can often do more for unbelievers than can priests, monks or nuns. It is easier for them to form relationships and friendships with them, to come into contact and mingle among them. Priests, monks and nuns awaken mistrust in those non-Christians who believe deeply in their own religion and hold Christians in abhorrence. Priests and religious often lack a point of contact, having no opportunities to meet unbelievers. Moreover, prudence and the rules of their foundations sometimes prevent them from going beyond certain limits of friendliness, from entering family homes or building up close relationships.

On the other hand, those who live in the world often have wide opportunities to enter into close relationships with unbelievers. Their occupations—administration, agriculture, commerce or whatever it may be—can, if they wish, bring them into touch with them continually. With the help of charity and the kindliness they themselves bring to these contacts, they can if they wish form true friendships that will open the most firmly closed of homes to them. The role of the brothers and sisters who are neither priests nor religious is not the instruction of unbelievers in the Christian religion and the bringing about of their conversion; rather it is one of preparation, by leading unbelievers to hold them in esteem by freeing them of their prejudices, by the example of their lives, and by teaching them Christian morality more by their actions than by their words. Thus by gaining their affection, confidence and close friendship, they will move their minds in such a way that missionaries will find the ground prepared for them and minds well disposed, willing to go to the missionaries themselves or to be easily approached by them.

The duty of evangelizing unbelievers is incumbent upon the faithful of Christian lands. Any hesitation and coldness of heart on their part in the fulfilling of a duty so grave (because it concerns the salvation of souls) and so pressing (because death is carrying so many before the supreme court of justice every day) is a responsibility of which everyone will have to carry his due share. Time is given us so we may sanctify ourselves and save others, and not so we may be useless and wicked. We must heed Jesus' grave warning: "Every idle word that men shall speak, they shall render an account for it in the day of judgment." [43]

If God allows some people to pile up riches instead of making themselves poor as Jesus did, it is so that they may use what he has entrusted to them as loyal servants, in accordance with the Master's will, to do spiritual and temporal good to others, giving their material resources where they are needed for the accomplishment of some spiritual good. They will have to render account for the good they might have done but failed to do. Jesus said so very often in the Gospels: "Love one another . . . do unto another as you would he should do unto you . . . love your neighbor as yourself." If after having read, heard and meditated on these words so often, the faithful and especially priests, monks

[43] Matt: 12:36.

and nuns—who by the nature of their lives should be wholly devoted to the people among whom they live—neglect and desert
these distant souls in their great and extreme danger, they can
expect nothing but grave reproof for so grave a dereliction from
him who said: "As long as you did it not to one of these least,
neither did you do it to me."

In the twentieth century the evangelization of unbelieving nations has become more than ever the strict duty of Christian
nations. In former times ignorance about the countries they in-
habited, the extreme length of journeys and the great difficulty
of communications, the impossibility of entering into relationships with fanatical or savage peoples who expelled or martyred
all missionaries and often all Europeans, were sufficient excuses
for delays in preaching the Gospel. These excuses no longer exist
today. The longest journeys have become short and easy. Non-
Christian nations are for the most part subject to Europeans, and
the others are compelled to respect them. All over the world,
wherever there are non-Christians, there is contact between them
and Europeans, and a missionary can go wherever he will. He
cannot always call himself a missionary openly, but he can conceal
what he is under the guise of trade, agriculture, or something of
the kind.

Our native land is an extension of our family. By making the
members of our families closer to us than others in our lives, God
has given us special duties towards them. The same is true of our
compatriots, and consequently also of the colonies of our native
country, which form part of the great family of our nation. This
incontestable and very powerful argument tells us the primary reason why we should work especially for the conversion of the
unbelievers in the colonies of our native land. There is another:
if we neglect them, it is to be feared they will be totally abandoned.
As they belong to our native land, the Christians of other coun-

tries will not concern themselves about them, but will leave them in our charge.

The conversion of unbelievers is often very difficult, especially when the local government puts obstacles in the way and is opposed to the Catholic religion. This ought not to be any kind of discouragement—on the contrary, it should make us work more zealously, on the grounds that the obstacles show that a greater effort is needed. Whatever sort of unbelievers they may be, they are no more difficult to convert than the Romans and barbarians of the first Christian centuries. However strongly opposed to the Church the governments of their countries may be, they cannot be more opposed to it than were Nero and his successors. If the brothers and sisters have the same zeal for souls and the same virtues as the Christians of the first centuries, they will accomplish the same good works. Like them, they will do secretly and in disguise the good they cannot do openly. Love will reveal the means to them, and Jesus will make fruitful the endeavors he inspires. Let me repeat: "We must not measure our labors by our weakness, but our efforts by our tasks." If the difficulties are great, we must hasten that much more quickly to put ourselves to work and increase our efforts that much the more.[44]

The following extracts from his letters show the high hopes in the heart of Brother Charles at that time.

Do not be surprised by the storms of this time. St. Peter's ship has seen many another. Think of the evening of the day when St. Peter and St. Paul were martyred. How black everything must have looked to the little community of Christians at Rome! But the first Christians were not discouraged. How petty then hell's

[44] From a letter to the Abbé Caron dated March 11, 1909 (cf. ES, p. 260–66).

present endeavors ought to seem to us with nineteen centuries of the life of the Church to strengthen our faith. Jesus said that they "would not prevail." . . . Blessing us, Jesus said as much to us as to the apostles: "Go, preach the Gospel to every creature." We, too, can "do all things in him who strengtheneth" us: "He has overcome the world." Like him, we shall always have the cross; like him, we shall always be persecuted; like him, we shall, ultimately, always triumph, in proportion to our loyalty to his grace and insofar as we let him live in us and act in and through us. We are with the Almighty, and our enemies have only the power it pleases him to give them to exercise and sanctify us, so that his Church and his elect may win the only true and everlasting victories, the victories of the spirit.

. . . But let us return to the Gospel; if we are not living the Gospel, Jesus is not living in us. Let us return to poverty and Christian simplicity. What struck me most during those few days in France after nineteen years away was the advances made by the taste for costly vanities, and their appearance among all classes of society, even among the most Christian families, together with a great lack of depth and an addiction to worldly and frivolous distractions completely out of place in times as grave as these, in times of persecution, and in no way in harmony with the Christian life. The danger lies *in us,* not in our enemies. All our enemies can do is present us with victories. Evil can reach us only from within ourselves. The remedy lies in a return to the Gospel.[45]

＊

How I should like to see the faithful Christians of France give a little attention to the population of Algeria, for they have

[45] From a letter to the Abbé Caron, dated June 30, 1909 (cf. ES, pp. 239 ff.).

parental duties towards their children—and this is a French land, dying in Mohammedanism! [46]

*

May Jesus make 1910 a year of graces for the Sahara! This land, these souls, have been waiting for the Gospel for nineteen hundred years.[47]

*

I shall do what I can, and God will do what he wills. Pray for me, asking that my life may be such that he can use me to do a little good. Whatever happens, if I am good, my journey through this world will be of value to souls; if I am wicked or lukewarm, I shall do nothing well and nothing good will be done through me.[48]

*

How true it is that only Jesus deserves to be loved passionately.[49]

*

Yes, indeed, Jesus suffices. Where he is, nothing is lacking. Precious as they may be in whom there shines a reflection of him,

[46] From a letter to his cousin, Madame de Bondy, dated July 31, 1909 (cf. TPF, p. 227).

[47] From a letter to Mgr. Guérin, dated October 31, 1909 (cf. ES, p. 241).

[48] From another letter to Mgr. Guérin, dated February 4, 1910 (cf. ES, p. 242).

[49] From a letter to the Abbé Caron, dated July 16, 1910 (*ibid. loc. cit*).

he is still our All. He is everything in time and in eternity. How fortunate we are to have an All nothing can steal from us and who will always be ours unless we ourselves leave him.[50]

For the fulfillment of his plan for the apostolate, Brother Charles required that one undergo a very profound conversion. On July 24, 1914 he wrote to one Joseph Hours, who was thinking of joining him in his plans for the apostolate of the Union of the Brothers and Sisters of the Sacred Heart: [51]

There is always work to be done by example, goodness and prayer. We can enter into closer relationships with souls that are lukewarm or estranged from the faith, so as to lead them gradually, by the power of our patience, gentleness and goodness, by the influence of virtue rather than advice, back to a more Christian life or to the faith itself. By entering into friendly relationships with people totally opposed to religion we can, by our goodness and virtue, destroy their prejudices and bring them completely to God. We should enlarge our acquaintanceship both with good Christians, so as to be sustained in the fiery love of God, and with non-practising Christians, seeking to establish with them not worldly social relations, but the bonds of cordial friendship, so as to lead them to esteem and trust us, and thus to reconcile them with our faith. One has to be as much a missionary in France as in a country of unbelievers, and being so is the duty of us all, priests and lay people, men and women.[52]

In July 1914, in the course of a very skilled forensic analysis of the lack of faith of the young people of his time and an unhappy

[50] From a letter to Mgr. Guérin, dated November 1, 1910 (*ibid. loc. cit.*).
[51] Cf. IS, p. 356, and for this apostolate, IS, pp. 350 ff.
[52] Cf. IS, p. 356.

acknowledgement of the class-war then being waged, he gave further precise instructions:

By the simplicity and moderation of our lives and our endeavors to be an inspiration to those around us, we must fight with the weapon of Christian brotherhood in all our relationships, to fill in the trench being dug by class differences. . . . I do not think much needs to be said or written; we must reform ourselves, and reform those close to us, trying in a gentle and friendly way to reform those over whom we have influence, and trying to extend that influence in an attempt to extend the range of the reform. Above all, we must work perseveringly, without becoming discouraged, remembering that the struggle against ourselves, the world and the devil will last until the end of time. Action, prayer and suffering are our three tools.[53]

The war prevented him from visiting France in the summer of 1915. A few months before his death he wrote:

I am thinking more than ever about the little work, the little Confraternity of which you have seen the statutes—or rather, the projected statutes. But I am thinking of simplifying its organization before I publish it. My intention is to stay in France after the war for as long as is necessary to start the work going there.[54]

We know nothing of the changes Brother Charles wanted to make in the association. They cannot have been very important, for his ideas remained essentially unchanged in 1916, if we may judge by the following letter written in April:

[53] From a letter to Joseph Hours, dated July 14, 1914 (cf. IS, pp. 356 ff.).

[54] From a letter to his cousin, Madame de Bondy, dated July 31, 1916 (cf. TPS, p. 286).

All Christians ought to be like Priscilla and Aquila.[55] You and I will pray together, asking God that they may be. "Love one another, as I have loved you . . . By this shall all men know that you are my disciples." As I have loved you: the Divine Master loved us by working for the salvation of our souls and this is how we ought to love one another. One another means every soul, for "You are all brothers . . . You all have one Father, who is in heaven." Let us behave like Priscilla and Aquila. We must concern ourselves with those around us, those we know, anyone close to us, using the best means with each individually—words with one, silence with another, the power of example, goodness and brotherly love with all, "becoming all things to all men" to win all for Jesus. Both speech and silence are being used today.[56]

Two months before his death, Brother Charles briefly described the fundamental spirit and chief guiding principles of his association:

There must be Priscillas and Aquilas united among themselves in their individual and collective activities and knowing one another well, each in the mystical priesthood of the faithful soul offering itself and Jesus for all the intentions of the Divine Saviour (the glory of God, the coming of his kingdom, the fulfillment of his will, the salvation of souls), and like Jesus making the salvation of mankind his life's work.[57]

In the year of his death, 1916, Charles de Foucauld briefly noted down references and ideas that impressed him in the course of reading Holy Scripture, the Imitation of Christ *and the Lives of the Saints. They no longer take the form of lengthy meditations,*

---

[55] Cf. Acts 18:2 ff; Rom. 16:3; I Cor. 16:9.
[56] From a letter to Joseph Hours, dated April 28, 1916 (cf. IS, p. 358).
[57] From a letter to Joseph Hours, October 1, 1916 (cf. IS, p. 358).

as at Nazareth, but are short, much abbreviated sentences. They are all stamped with the impress of his love for Jesus and his great longing to work with him in the redemption of men.[58]

January 1916

1. *Gospel:* Jesus meant his name "Saviour" to symbolize his life's work, the salvation of souls. In imitation of our only Model, our life's work should be the salvation of souls.
   Imit. 2:9: We should prefer God's good pleasure to human consolations.
   Lives of the Saints: The Circumcision: May the name of Jesus be always in our hearts and on our lips in this life, and may it be our consolation and hope at the hour of our death.
2. *Gospel:* In every human being, see a soul to be *saved.*
   Imit. 2:9: May every grace make us more humble when we realize how lilttle we have deserved it, and how little loyalty there is in us.
   Lives of the Saints: St. Macarius: We should be devoted wholly to God alone. Everything else is nothing in comparison with God.
3. *Gospel:* Jesus came into the world preaching peace: for the penitent, the peace of the remission of sins, the peace of grace, so that they might not sin again; let us do penance with pure hearts.
   Imit. 2:10: Render to God the things that are God's: the grace and goodness within you. Impute to yourselves what is yours: the sin and evil within you.
   St. Genevieve: The only way of doing any real good is by sanctifying yourself. St. Genevieve, protect France! Make the spirit of poverty, humility, purity, charity and faith reign here.
4. *Gospel:* In the very moment he was given the name Jesus,

[58] Only selections from these notes have previously been published. See OS, pp. 331–6.

"Saviour," our Lord poured out his blood, showing that it is by blood and suffering offered to God that souls are saved.

Imit. 2:10: Everything that happens to us is either done or permitted by God for the sake of our salvation: everything must contribute to our sanctification.

St. Gregory of Langres: Zeal for souls, prayer and penance.

5. *Gospel:* Like the Magi let us follow the star, grace, with urgency and loyalty. Let us follow the yearning given us by God by giving obedience to his representatives.

   Imit. 2:11: Serve God for God's sake alone; abandon everything, even yourself, and take the lowest place.

   St. Simeon Stylites: In comparison with God, the whole universe is nothing. The only thing necessary is to follow the yearning given us by God by obeying his representatives.

6. *Gospel:* Let us offer the whole of our lives to God, as the threefold gift of the Magi: the gold of love, the incense of prayer, and the myrrh of mortification; all three are always indispensable.

   Imit. 2:12: Deny yourselves, take up your cross and follow Jesus.

   The Epiphany: Pray and work for the conversion of all nations to the Christian faith.

7. *Gospel:* When one has seen Jesus, one has to go back by another way, the way of conversion, and not by the path of past mistakes.

   Imit. 2:12: If anyone will follow in my footsteps, let him deny himself, take up my cross and follow me.

   St. Lucius: We must inform ourselves about the Christian verities and enlarge our knowledge of them. We must be not only enlightened Christians, but also apostles.

8. *Gospel:* Our Lord came into the world from *charity,* in order to save by way of *self-abnegation,* coming to those he wanted to save in *humility,* making himself a man—he, who was God.

Imit. 3:1: Renounce everything. Concern yourself with pleasing your Creator, and with being loyal to him.

St. Apollinarius of Hierapolis: Be afraid of only one thing—sin.

9. *Gospel:* Our Lord was born in poverty and lowliness, and forgotten by men.

   Imit. 3:2: Books show the way, but it is God who, by grace, makes them understood and gives us strength to go on.

   St. Julian the Hospitaller: Avoid egotism. Live for God and your neighbor.

10. *Gospel:* Our Lord in his manger teaches gentleness, availability to all, and close fellowship with lowly and unsophisticated people.

    Imit. 3:3: The world promises very little, and even that is transitory, yet men serve it passionately; God promises great and eternal rewards, but the hearts of men are not touched.

    St. William of Bourges: Spend your life in the love of God and your neighbor, in fulfilling the divine will, in prayer, charitable works and mortification.

11. *Gospel:* Our Lord in his manger teaches us mortification by embracing suffering, the companion of poverty and self-emptying, by himself becoming a poor weak child.

    Imit. 3:3: God comes to his elect in two ways, by temptation and consolation.

    St. Theodore the Cenobite, Abbot: We must quietly follow God's call in the various estates he has chosen for us: as pilgrims, hermits, cenobites, hospitallers—all in unchanging interior perfection.

12. *Gospel:* Our Lord in his manger teaches us to go even to souls that reject and desert us, and to stop among them, patiently and perseveringly.

    Imit. 3:3: O Lord, teach me to do your will; teach me to live a lowly life, worthy of you.

St. Alfred of Scotland, Abbot: "No one ever saw him angry; his words and actions bore the gentle imprint of the unction and peace that filled his soul."

13. *Gospel:* To be worthy of the kingdom of heaven and of Jesus, have the purity of soul and innocency of a little child.

   Imit. 3:4: Remember your sins with much pain, and never think you have changed because of some good action you have done.

   St. Veronica of Binasco (or Milan): How much more a beam of divine enlightenment teaches us than does all human wisdom.

14. *Gospel:* Jesus revealed himself first to the shepherds: the divine light—the "true light"—enlightens souls in proportion to their *purity,* not according to the measure of their intellect or knowledge. We must be pure of soul and humble.

   Imit. 3:4: The truth is that you are nothing but a sinner, subject to many passions and bound by them.

   St. Hilary: Be afraid of only one thing in the world: not loving Jesus enough.

15. *Gospel:* Jesus in the cave at Bethlehem teaches us to remain silent and withdrawn in solitude whenever we are not called out of it by his will.

   Imit. 3:4: May nothing be as great, valuable, admirable or important in your eyes as the things that are eternal.

   St. Paul the Hermit: Here was a true hermit, living in almost continual prayer, extreme penance, extreme poverty and complete solitude.

16. *Gospel:* We can wrap our Lord in swaddling clothes no less truly than did the Blessed Virgin: we do it when we clothe a poor person for love of him. "As long as you did it to one of these my least brethren, you did it unto me."

   Imit. 3:4: Do not question the works of God, but plumb the depths of your own iniquities, the wrong you have so often done, and the good you have left undone.

St. Honoratus, Bishop of Arles: Work in the situation in which you find yourself, for the salvation of souls and the glory of God. Anyone trying to represent charity in human form would inevitably paint a portrait of Honoratus.

17. *Gospel:* Our Lord's mother was a virgin, his foster-father was the chaste St. Joseph; his precursor was to be St. John the Baptist, a virgin, and his dearest apostle the virgin St. John. Such are the rewards of chastity.

    Imit. 3:4: The Spirit of Truth teaches us to scorn transitory things and love what eternally endures, to forget the world and long for heaven.

    St. Anthony, Abbot: We must prepare our souls for battle, and defy the devil.

18. *Gospel:* Jesus is our elder brother. Let us live, think, speak and act as the younger brothers of Jesus, living with him and Mary and Joseph.

    Imit. 3:5: Tear the inordinate affections out of my heart, that healed and purified, I may become fit to love you, strong in suffering and firm in perseverance.

    St. Peter's Chair at Rome: God builds on nothing. It was by his death that Jesus saved the world; it was on the nothingness of the apostles that he founded his Church; it is by sanctity and in the nothingness of human means that heaven is gained and the faith propagated.

19. *Gospel:* Like Mary and Joseph, we must do everything Jesus wills, and find time to contemplate him silently and adore him, for this too is his will.

    Imit. 3:5: Nothing is better or more perfect than love, for love is born of God, and can find rest only in God.

    St. Canute, King of Denmark: In everything, do what will

be most pleasing to Jesus, fearing nothing except not loving him enough and not doing his will.

20. *Gospel:* The life of Joseph and Mary after the birth of Jesus was one of perfect fulfillment of the ritual prayers and the whole religious law, tasks laid on them by Jesus, and contemplation of him whether with the eyes of the body or those of the spirit—hours spent in contemplating and adoring Jesus.

     Imit. 3:5: Love can do everything; it accomplishes many things that vainly tire and exhaust anyone who does not love.

     St. Sebastian: Have an ardent zeal for the sanctification of your neighbor.

21. *Gospel:* Mary and Joseph were with Jesus, constantly doing his will, while either looking at him or thinking about him.

     Imit. 3:5: Love is swift to act, sincere, devout, gentle, prudent, strong, patient, loyal, constant, magnanimous, and never self-seeking.

     St. Agnes: Suffer all things rather than fail to do Jesus' will.

22. *Gospel:* All things being equal in other respects, prefer lowliness to honor, desertion to a crowd, and penury to plenty, for the sake of being more like Jesus.

     Imit. 3:5: As soon as one begins to be self-seeking, one ceases to love.

     St. Vincent, Deacon and Martyr: By grace the martyrs triumphed over the rack, iron nails and gridirons; should we not overcome small temptation with the same grace?

23. *Gospel:* All things being equal in other respects, prefer to be weak rather than strong, scorned than idolized, rejected than sought after, so as to be more like Jesus.

     Imit. 3:5: Love is circumspect, humble, direct, and neither soft nor frivolous; it does not concern itself with vanities; it is sober, chaste, firm, tranquil, and keeps a careful watch on the senses.

     St. Raymond of Penafort: The more graces one receives, the more vigilant over oneself one should be, to avoid the least imperfection.

24. *Gospel:* All things being equal in other respects, prefer solitude to company, silence to speech, the hidden life to life in the society of others, for the sake of being more like Jesus.

    Imit. 3:5: Anyone who is not willing to suffer everything and abandon himself utterly to the will of the beloved, does not know what it is to love.

    St. Timothy: Be an example to the faithful in your conversation, your behavior, your charity, faith and chastity.

25. *Gospel:* Have the greatest devotion to the Holy Eucharist, where our Lord is really present as he was in the manger.

    Imit. 3:6: Think less of the lover's gift than of the giver's love. Be more moved by the affection than by the benefit bestowed.

    The Conversion of St. Paul: "Lord, what wilt thou have me do?" May our whole lives echo St. Paul's cry.

26. *Gospel:* Keep some hours for pure adoration and contemplation of Jesus, as Mary and Joseph did at Bethlehem and Nazareth.

    Imit. 3:6: If weakness makes us fall, we should take greater courage, hope more in grace, and protect ourselves from vain complacency and pride.

    St. Polycarp: Live holily in order to die holily. By daily victories over the smallest temptations, prepare to triumph over the greatest.

27. *Gospel:* Our Lord came down to the manger to save souls: he is teaching us to make the salvation of souls our life's work for God's sake: the fulfillment of the two commandments to love God and our neighbor.

    Imit. 3:7: It is better to be humble though of limited intellect and insight, than to be learned and self-satisfied.

    St. John Chrysostom: Fulfill the divine will by prayer, penance and purity of soul, making yourself a good instrument, fit for use by God.

28. *Gospel:* I really am always with Jesus, Mary and Joseph: I must remind myself of this constantly, thinking, speaking and acting in accordance with this belief.

    Imit. 3:7: Virtue consists in being genuinely humble and charitable, in seeking only the glory of God, in being convinced of one's own nothingness, in sincerely despising oneself, and in preferring humiliation to honor.

    St. Cyril of Alexandria: We must distrust ourselves when we are judging others.

29. *Gospel:* The aim of our lives should be the salvation of souls for God's sake, the salvation of our own souls and the souls of our neighbors. Souls are saved by sanctity, sacrifice, example and words.

    Imit. 3:8: In his generous and infinite goodness, God never ceases doing good even to the ungrateful, among whom I am one. We should imitate him, doing good to the ungrateful, and being grateful, humble and fervent ourselves.

    St. Francis de Sales: How good God must be since his servant was so good! . . . If you overdo anything, let it be gentleness.

30. *Gospel:* Jesus in his manger has watched me at every moment of my life. Similarly, he can see me from the tabernacle. In this belief, I ought to do at all times what would be most pleasing to him.

    Imit. 3:9: We should rejoice only in God, and hope only in God, for God alone is good.

    St. Bathilde, Queen of France: Pray to St. Bathilde for France.

31. *Gospel:* Kneeling with the Blessed Virgin and St. Joseph at Jesus' feet, we should love him, obey him, imitate him, in everything do what would please him most, working with all our strength for the salvation of souls.

    Imit. 3:10: In these ways you have shown me your love: I was not, and you created me; I strayed far from you, and you brought me back to follow you and bade me love you.

St. Marcella, Widow: Love sacred reading. Instruct yourself unremittingly in the science of salvation.

February 1916

1. *Gospel:* By the divine mercy, Jesus came into the world, infinitely loving God, justice, truth and goodness. He teaches us to love God above all things, to obey him in all things and to love our neighbors as ourselves for love of God.

   Imit. 3:10: God, who ought to be served by all things, has deigned himself to serve me, giving himself to me in the Eucharist and longing to give himself to me eternally in heaven.

   St. Ignatius, Martyr: With what strength and love the martyrs suffered such torments! Have not I the strength and love to overcome my daily wretched little temptations?

2. *Gospel:* Jesus did all things perfectly, according to the will of God: he gives us an example by his perfect fulfillment of all the ceremonial laws although he himself was not bound by them, so as to teach us the necessity of being very faithful to them.

   Imit. 3:10: Man finds true freedom and holiness in the service of God.

   The Purification: Candlemas: We should religiously observe the laws of Christianity in their least details. We should love the light of candles as symbolizing the light of Christ; the wax symbolizes his body, the wick his soul, the flame his divinity.

3. *Gospel:* The Flight into Egypt: Do the will of God whatever demands it makes, unhesitatingly and despite the apparent impossibility of the death of the senses it involves.

   Imit. 3:11: Your desires are often inflamed and carry you

impetuously away: but think whether the motive of this ardor is my glory or your own benefit. If it is I who am within you, you will be satisfied with what I ordain; but if you are self-seeking, failure will worry you and bring you down.

St. Blaise, Bishop of Sebaste: Pray to the saints for your temporal needs, and even more for your spiritual ones. These friends and fathers, whose hearts are full of charity, will help you.

4. *Gospel:* Jesus came into the world, deserted and despised; soon afterwards, he was persecuted. We must give our attention to abandonment, scorn and persecution, and rejoice if we succeed in sharing them with Jesus.

   Imit. 3:11: Not every impulse that seems good should be followed at once, nor ought we to reject immediately what is repugnant to us.

   St. Joan of Valois, Queen of France: St. Joan and all the saints of France, pray for France!

5. *Gospel:* We should obey like the Holy Family. A sudden command in the middle of the night leading to something almost impossible: a long journey on foot through dangerous deserts in the middle of winter; immediate obedience and faith in God who gives us the means of doing what he commands.

   Imit. 3:11: Sometimes the most holy zeal and the best desires must be moderated until it is possible to see the will of God clearly, for sometimes the spirit of darkness disguises itself as an angel of light.

   The Holy Martyrs of Japan: Pray for the conversion of Japan and work there if possible. Ask God to teach us to sacrifice ourselves for his sake.

6. *Gospel:* When on the course of a journey we suffer from cold, inclement weather, hunger or fatigue, or if we are in

danger, we must make an act of union with Jesus fleeing into Egypt, and thank him for letting us suffer with him.

Imit. 3:12: Endure present evils patiently for God's sake, and so avoid eternal torments.

St. Dorothea of Caesarea, Virgin and Martyr: Keep a pure heart and you will become capable of the greatest virtues and sacrifices.

7. *Gospel:* We owe immediate and perfect obedience to all God's wishes, whatever might be the difficulty, suffering or apparent impossibility involved.

Imit. 3:12: Like a dumb animal, for the poor pleasures of this mortal life you incur the death of the soul.

St. Romauld: Do not let a day go by without some physical acts of penance. The soul benefits from what the body is denied: *Doctrina sanctorum omnium.*[59]

8. *Gospel:* As soon as we realize God wants us to do something, we should do it without the least delay, with all our heart and strength.

Imit. 3:12: Temptations will go on until the end of life: our weapons are prayer, work, prudence and obedience.

St. John of Matha: Be kind and compassionate, let no distress leave you untouched. See Jesus in every human being. Do unto another as you would have him do unto you.

9. *Gospel:* When we are tired, cold, hungry, on exhausting journeys, in difficulties or dangers, we should unite ourselves with Jesus on the flight into Egypt; happy to suffer with him, at one with him in our souls, wanting what he wanted, offering ourselves for what he offered himself.

Imit. 3:13: Jesus became obedient and humble, making himself the least of all in order to overcome our pride and teach us obedience and humility.

[59] "Teaching of all the saints."

St. Apollonia of Alexandria, Virgin and Martyr: Never serve God calculatingly, but sacrifice yourself unhesitatingly.

10. *Gospel:* We must give absolute, immediate and perfect obedience to all God's wishes, in spite of difficulties, our repugnance or the apparent impossibility of the task.

    Imit. 3:13: Son of nothingness, what have you to complain of? Wretched sinner, what answer can you make when they reproach you—you who have so often offended God and deserved hell?

    St. Scholastica: Everything except God, souls, heaven and hell is transitory. All that is necessary, the only worthwhile and lasting thing, is doing the will of God with all our strength.

11. *Gospel:* As soon as Jesus comes to us, we should expect persecution and suffering. Just as Jesus was persecuted and suffered in this world, so too the faithful soul and the Church will be persecuted and will suffer.

    Imit. 3:13: You have often deserved hell, but God has spared you so that you may thereby acknowledge his love.

    St. Benedict of Aniana, Abbot: Be hard on yourself and indulgent towards others.

12. *Gospel:* The Flight into Egypt. At all times, do wholeheartedly what God wills—but do it as Mary and Joseph did, with their eyes constantly fixed on Jesus and their souls always united with him.

    Imit. 3:14: Seemingly praiseworthy men have fallen as low as it is possible to fall: neither holiness nor wisdom, strength nor chastity last unendingly without Your help.

    St. Ludans: Only one thing is necessary: to love God with your whole heart and do his will.

13. *Gospel—The Flight into Egypt:* In all situations and places, and at all times, Jesus is our Saviour, offering himself for the salvation of souls, working and suffering for the salvation of

souls, taking action for the salvation of souls. We must do the same.

Imit. 3:14: Knowing all my sins as I do, how can I be proud? How can I be puffed up by the praises of others, who are and know nothing, and will vanish along with their words?

St. Catherine of Ricci (Florentine Dominican): When we consider the virtues and love of the saints, we must humiliate ourselves and be converted: what they could do, we can do. God never fails men.

14. *Gospel:* Doing the will of God means striving to do what God commands: if he—who can do everything—wishes us to succeed, he will give us success.

Imit. 3:15: In everything you feel you ought to do, say: Lord, may this be done if it is your will, for it is difficult to decide whether it is the Spirit of goodness, the evil one or one's own mind that has inspired a desire.

St. Valentine, Martyr: Make good use of every opportunity to enlighten your neighbor and communicate some good thing to him.

15. *Gospel:* When God commands us to do something, he wants us to make every endeavor to do it, while reserving to himself our success or failure, in accordance with the purpose of his wisdom.

Imit. 3:15: Whenever anything presents itself to the mind as desirable, long for it and ask God for it, humbly saying always: Not my will, but yours!

Sts. Faustinus and Jovita, Martyrs: Remember that it is the duty of every Christian to follow his Master to Calvary.

16. *Gospel:* Absolute and perfect obedience to all God's known wishes!

Imit. 3:15: Grant that I may always want and will what is most pleasing to you and what you love most.

St. Juliana of Nicomedia, Martyr: The martyrs have suffered such torments for God, and I cannot overcome such weak temptations!

17. *Gospel:* We should expect conflict, persecution, exile, difficulties, poverty, humiliation, suffering and extreme fatigues, for what was Jesus' lot will certainly be ours. We should endure them joyfully, in union with Jesus and making his intentions our own.

    Imit. 3:15: May your will be mine; may my will always follow yours, and never deviate from it.

    St. Sylvanus, Bishop (born at Toulouse): Before giving advice to others, give them the example of your virtues.

18. *Gospel:* Whenever Jesus comes to someone, the cross comes with him: when he entered Mary's womb, he brought St. Joseph anxiety about her holy childbearing. When he comes into the world, he brings persecution and exile.

    Imit. 3:15: Being united with you, let me will only what you will!

    St. Simeon, Bishop of Jerusalem: May our life be hidden with Jesus in God. We should seek to please God, to love him and to be loved by him—and not to please the world and be acclaimed by it.

19. *Gospel:* Through Jesus' stay in Egypt, God poured out graces on that country, preparing it for its future conversion. Jesus' stay anywhere is a source of graces there; graces are poured out there, effecting and preparing the way for the salvation of souls.

    Imit. 3:15: Grant that I may die to all worldly things and like to be forgotten and despised in this world for your sake.

    St. Barbatus, Bishop of Benevento: The sacrifices of apostolic zeal are never lost; sooner or later God's glory profits by them. We should never be discouraged by lack of success.

20. *Gospel:* The Flight into Egypt. Christian parents, your chil-

dren will be crosses to you. After offering them to God, as Mary and Joseph did, expect to receive more pains than pleasure from them.

Imit. 3:15: Grant me rest in you exceeding what man can desire, and grant that my heart may seek peace in you alone.

St. Eucherius, Bishop of Orleans: We should entrust the purity of our souls and bodies to Mary.

21. *St. Severinus, Bishop and Martyr; St. Pepin of Landen, Mayor of the Palace.*

22. *Gospel:* Flight into Egypt. How did the Holy Family live in Egypt? An interior life of love and admiration for Jesus, and of obedience to and union with Jesus. An exterior life of extreme poverty, difficulties, lowliness and labor.

Imit. 3:16: No temporal good could satisfy you, because you were not created to enjoy it.

St. Margaret of Cortona, Penitent.—St. Peter's Chair at Antioch: Make good past sins by conversion and penance. How greatly God blessed the remorse of the saints—and to what a large degree it was inspired by him.

23. *Gospel:* Obedience and union with the will of God, whatever it may be, striving in all circumstances to do it most perfectly.

Imit. 3:16: May our consolation be to rejoice in the infinite blessedness of God, loving him above all things.

St. Serenus, Gardener and Martyr.—St. Peter Damian: Remember the purity of the saints: the purity of Jesus, born of the Blessed Virgin, brought up by St. Joseph, heralded by St. John the Baptist. We must make every endeavor to bring others to purity.

24. *Gospel:* We should do always what is most pleasing to Jesus, keeping our gaze fixed on him continually, as did Mary and Joseph.

Imit. 3:17: If you do not reject me and take my name out of the book of life, no tribulation can befall me.

St. Matthias, Apostle.—Blessed Robert of Arbriselle: Be generous with God; never think you have done enough for his glory.

25. *St. Tarasius, Bishop of Constantinople.*
26. *St. Leander, Bishop of Seville.*
27. *St. Porphyrius, Bishop of Gaza.*
28. *Sts. Romanus and Lupicianus, Abbots (Diocese of Belley):* Be firm but gentle, keeping severity principally for yourself.

March 1916

1. *St. Albinus, Bishop of Angers:* Be ready to make any sacrifice for the relief of your neighbor's lot: "As long as you did it to one of these my least brethren, you did it to me."
2. *Blessed Henry Suso:* Live in the continual presence of Jesus, and in devout intimacy with him.

June 1916

11. *Pentecost—John 14:23:* "If anyone loves me, he will keep my word." Our first duty is to love God. How do we obey God? By obeying his word.
12. *Luke 1:15:* "He shall drink no wine nor strong drink": God is teaching us through his angel that detachment from material pleasures disposes us to receive divine grace.
13. *Luke 1:31:* "Thou shalt call his name Jesus." The name Jesus ("Saviour") symbolizes our Lord's work. If we would imitate him, we should do his work. We must consecrate our lives to the salvation of souls, saving them by the proper means given to each of us in accordance with God's will.

14. *Luke 1:39–56:* "Mary . . . went into the hill country with haste." When one is filled with Jesus, one is full of charity. One goes to those one would save, as Jesus went to them in becoming incarnate; one does so with haste, because charity is pressing and will brook no delay. Let us work for the salvation of souls, going to them in great haste: haste might save some souls, prevent some sins, produce some additional merits. Slowness in well-doing in behalf of the beloved is incompatible with love.

15. *Luke 1:57; 2:7:* "She . . . laid him in a manger, because there was no room for them in the inn." Poverty, lowliness, abandonment, humiliation: those were the signs among which you were born and by which you can be recognized. Make me love these signs, wearing them as often as need be for your glory, for the good of my soul or the souls of others, for the fulfillment of your will. Make me happy to bear them myself and venerate them in others.

17. *Luke 2:8–20:* "There were in the same country shepherds." The first worshippers, the first company it pleased our Lord to have at his manger, were the most humble, unsophisticated, unimportant and simple people—shepherds.

He did not merely accept them: he called them, having them called by pure spirits, the angels, their superiors in purity, intellect, love, and power.

We should have infinite regard for the most unimportant, humble and unsophisticated people, our brothers, honoring them as Jesus' intimates, realizing that they deserve to be, for they are generally the simplest and purest people, least wrapped in pride. We should mix with them and so far as God wills, be one of them. We should do all possible for their bodies and souls, treating them with honor for the honor of Jesus, and fraternally, so as to have the honor and good fortune of being reckoned one of them. Unhappy is he whose insensate pride despises those who God puts in the first ranks—"as long as you did it to one of these my least breathen, you did it to me."

18. *Luke 2:21:* "His name was called Jesus"—that is, "Saviour." It was his will that his name should be an expression of his work. The work of his life on earth, what he came down into this world to do, was saving men. If, as is our duty, we would imitate him, the first thing we must do is make the salvation of men our life's work, putting all our strength and our every effort into the task of saving souls, whatever our place in life may be.

Later our Lord was frequently to repeat the command he had given us to save souls by taking the name Jesus "Saviour": "Love God—this is the first commandment. And the second is to love your neighbor as yourself . . . Love one another as I have loved you. By this all men shall know that you are my disciples."

Loving our neighbor—that is, loving all human beings as we do ourselves—consists in making our life's work the salvation of both the souls of others and our own souls. Loving others as Jesus has loved us means making the salvation of all souls our life's work, if need be giving our blood for them, as Jesus did.

19. *Luke 2:49:* "Did you not know that I must be about my Father's business?" Our only business and occupation here below is the business of our heavenly Father, our true Father, our Creator, to whom all that we are and have belongs, whose rights over us and everything else are absolute. What is his business and occupation? The works it is his will that we should do at every moment of our lives are divine works with

three ends in common: his glory, the sanctification of our own souls, and the sanctification of the souls of others, our neighbors. Whenever our actions do not tend to the glorification of God, the salvation of our own souls or the souls of others, we are not working at our Father's business; we are stealing ourselves from him, stealing our time and the tools he has given us from him.

"He will require account of even the idle words you speak."

20. *Luke 2:50–51:* "and he went down with them, and came to Nazareth and was subject to them." [60] "He went down": his whole life was spent in "going down." He went down in the Incarnation, going down to be a small child, going down in obedience, in becoming poor, abandoned, exiled, persecuted, tortured, in always putting himself in the lowest place. "When thou art invited, go, sit down in the lowest place": it is what he did himself from the time of his coming into the feast of life till the time of his death. He came to Nazareth, the place of the hidden life, of ordinary family life: a life of prayer, work and obscurity, the silent virtues, practised with God, his close relations and his neighbors as its only witnesses. It was a humble, holy, obscure life of well-doing—the life of most human beings. For thirty years, he was our example of it. "He was subject to them": he, God, was subject to them, human beings, so becoming our example of obedience, humility and, in the real sense of the word, renunciation as infinite as his divinity.

21. *Luke 2:51–2:* "Jesus advanced in wisdom, and age, and grace." As he advanced in age, the wisdom and abundance of divine graces within him revealed themselves more and more, becoming ever more apparent to the outward eye in his external actions. It should be the same with us: the older

[60] Cf. Matt. 12:36.

we grow, the more apparent in our works should be the grace received in baptism, poured out on us in the sacraments, and given by God in ever increasing abundance to the faithful soul; every day of our lives should mark some advance in our wisdom and grace. If it is not so, we should weep and humble ourselves—especially if wrongdoing has made us fall back. But we should not be discouraged. To be checked or to fall back ought to make us more humble, more mistrustful of ourselves, more vigilant and indulgent, more full of goodness towards others, more gentle, humble and respectful, more brotherly towards our neighbor: it should make us penitent and more fully aware of our worthlessness and ingratitude—but also, forever infinitely confident in God and certain of his love. The fact that he loves us in spite of our worthlessness, should make us love him with a more tender and grateful love, saying to him every time we fall, as St. Peter did: "Yea, Lord, thou knowest that I love thee."

On July 15, 1916, Brother Charles wrote to Louis Massignon:

Love consists not in feeling that we love, but in wanting to love. We love above all things what we want to love above all things. If it comes about that we do succumb to a temptation, it is because our love is too weak, not because it does not exist. Like St. Peter, we should weep, like him we should repent and humble ourselves —but also like him, we should say three times: "I love you. I love you. You know that despite my weakness and sins, I love you."

As for Jesus' love for us, he has proved it to us clearly enough for us to believe in it without being able to feel it. To feel we loved him and he loved us would be heaven. But heaven is not, except at rare moments and in rare cases, for us here below.[61]

[61] Cf. IS, p. 362.

On December 1, 1916, the day of his death, he wrote to his cousin, Madame de Bondy:

How true it is that we shall never love enough. But God—who knows what clay he shaped us from and loves us more than a mother can her child—God, who does not lie,[62] has told us that he will not repulse anyone who comes to him.[63]

[62] Earlier French editions read here "who does not die"—clearly a copyist's error, reading "die" (*meurt*) for "lie" (*ment*).
[63] Cf. TPF, p. 292.

MEMENTO

The following sentences were written on the first page of a notebook Charles de Foucauld carried everywhere with him.

Live as though you were going to have to die as a martyr today.

The more we lack in this world, the more surely we discover the best thing the earth has to offer us: the cross.

The more firmly we embrace the cross, the more closely we are bound to Jesus, our Beloved, who is made fast to it.